Cuba

Other Books of Related Interest:

At Issue Series

Does the World Hate the United States?

Current Controversies

Espionage & Intelligence

Importing from China

Global Viewpoints

Capitalism

Civil Liberties

Poverty

Workers' Rights

Introducing Issues with Opposing Viewpoints

The Election Process

Opposing Viewpoints

Democracy

Poverty

"Congress shall make
no law ... abridging
the freedom of speech,
or of the press."

First Amendment to the US Constitution

The basic foundation of our democracy is the First Amendment guarantee of freedom of expression. The Opposing Viewpoints series is dedicated to the concept of this basic freedom and the idea that it is more important to practice it than to enshrine it.

Cuba

Noah Berlatsky, Book Editor

GREENHAVEN PRESS

A part of Gale, Cengage Learning

Detroit • New York • San Francisco • New Haven, Conn • Waterville, Maine • London

GALE
CENGAGE Learning·

Elizabeth Des Chenes, *Director, Publishing Solutions*

© 2013 Greenhaven Press, a part of Gale, Cengage Learning.

Gale and Greenhaven Press are registered trademarks used herein under license.

For more information, contact:
Greenhaven Press
27500 Drake Rd.
Farmington Hills, MI 48331-3535
Or you can visit our Internet site at gale.cengage.com

For product information and technology assistance, contact us at

Gale Customer Support, 1-800-877-4253
For permission to use material from this text or product, submit all requests online at
www.cengage.com/permissions

Further permissions questions can be emailed to permissionrequest@cengage.com

Articles in Greenhaven Press anthologies are often edited for length to meet page requirements. In addition, original titles of these works are changed to clearly present the main thesis and to explicitly indicate the author's opinion. Every effort is made to ensure that Greenhaven Press accurately reflects the original intent of the authors. Every effort has been made to trace the owners of copyrighted material.

Cover image copyright © yykkaa/Shutterstock.com.

LIBRARY OF CONGRESS CATALOGING-IN-PUBLICATION DATA

Cuba / Noah Berlatsky, book editor.
  p. cm. -- (Opposing viewpoints)
  Summary: "Opposing Viewpoints: Cuba: Opposing Viewpoints is the leading source for libraries and classrooms in need of current-issue materials. The viewpoints are selected from a wide range of highly respected sources and publications"-- Provided by publisher.
  Includes bibliographical references and index.
  ISBN 978-0-7377-6308-9 (hardback) -- ISBN 978-0-7377-6309-6 (paperback)
  1. Cuba. I. Berlatsky, Noah.
  F1758.C9486 2013
  972.91--dc23
                                                      2012040861

Printed in the United States of America
1 2 3 4 5 6 7 17 16 15 14 13

Contents

Chapter 3: What Is the Relationship Between Cuba Policy and US Domestic Politics?

Chapter 4: What Should Be the US Policy Toward Cuba?

Why Consider Opposing Viewpoints?

> *"The only way in which a human being can make some approach to knowing the whole of a subject is by hearing what can be said about it by persons of every variety of opinion and studying all modes in which it can be looked at by every character of mind. No wise man ever acquired his wisdom in any mode but this."*
>
> John Stuart Mill

In our media-intensive culture it is not difficult to find differing opinions. Thousands of newspapers and magazines and dozens of radio and television talk shows resound with differing points of view. The difficulty lies in deciding which opinion to agree with and which "experts" seem the most credible. The more inundated we become with differing opinions and claims, the more essential it is to hone critical reading and thinking skills to evaluate these ideas. Opposing Viewpoints books address this problem directly by presenting stimulating debates that can be used to enhance and teach these skills. The varied opinions contained in each book examine many different aspects of a single issue. While examining these conveniently edited opposing views, readers can develop critical thinking skills such as the ability to compare and contrast authors' credibility, facts, argumentation styles, use of persuasive techniques, and other stylistic tools. In short, the Opposing Viewpoints Series is an ideal way to attain the higher-level thinking and reading skills so essential in a culture of diverse and contradictory opinions.

In addition to providing a tool for critical thinking, Opposing Viewpoints books challenge readers to question their own strongly held opinions and assumptions. Most people form their opinions on the basis of upbringing, peer pressure, and personal, cultural, or professional bias. By reading carefully balanced opposing views, readers must directly confront new ideas as well as the opinions of those with whom they disagree. This is not to argue simplistically that everyone who reads opposing views will—or should—change his or her opinion. Instead, the series enhances readers' understanding of their own views by encouraging confrontation with opposing ideas. Careful examination of others' views can lead to the readers' understanding of the logical inconsistencies in their own opinions, perspective on why they hold an opinion, and the consideration of the possibility that their opinion requires further evaluation.

Evaluating Other Opinions

To ensure that this type of examination occurs, Opposing Viewpoints books present all types of opinions. Prominent spokespeople on different sides of each issue as well as well-known professionals from many disciplines challenge the reader. An additional goal of the series is to provide a forum for other, less known, or even unpopular viewpoints. The opinion of an ordinary person who has had to make the decision to cut off life support from a terminally ill relative, for example, may be just as valuable and provide just as much insight as a medical ethicist's professional opinion. The editors have two additional purposes in including these less known views. One, the editors encourage readers to respect others' opinions—even when not enhanced by professional credibility. It is only by reading or listening to and objectively evaluating others' ideas that one can determine whether they are worthy of consideration. Two, the inclusion of such viewpoints encourages the important critical thinking skill of objectively evaluating an author's credentials and bias. This evaluation will illuminate an author's reasons for taking a particular stance on an issue and will aid in readers' evaluation of the author's ideas.

It is our hope that these books will give readers a deeper understanding of the issues debated and an appreciation of the complexity of even seemingly simple issues when good and honest people disagree. This awareness is particularly important in a democratic society such as ours in which people enter into public debate to determine the common good. Those with whom one disagrees should not be regarded as enemies but rather as people whose views deserve careful examination and may shed light on one's own.

Thomas Jefferson once said that "difference of opinion leads to inquiry, and inquiry to truth." Jefferson, a broadly educated man, argued that "if a nation expects to be ignorant and free . . . it expects what never was and never will be." As individuals and as a nation, it is imperative that we consider the opinions of others and examine them with skill and discernment. The Opposing Viewpoints series is intended to help readers achieve this goal.

David L. Bender and Bruno Leone,
Founders

Introduction

"What makes it difficult for Batista is, of course, his unpopularity. He is despised."

*—1958 diary entry by
US Senator Allen J. Ellender,
referring to Cuban President
Fulgencio Batista's standing in Cuba,
quoted in Lars Schoultz,*
That Infernal Little Cuban Republic:
The United States and the
Cuban Revolution

For more than fifty years, Cuba has been controlled by an authoritarian Communist regime led by Fidel Castro, and for the last few years, by his brother, Raúl Castro.

Before the Cuban revolution of 1959, however, Cuba was ruled by Fulgencio Batista. Batista, who came from a poor farming family, joined the army and became a sergeant. He helped organize an army coup of the democratic government in 1933. He controlled the country from behind the scenes for several years and then was elected president himself in 1940. Upon the end of his term in 1944, he traveled and lived abroad. He orchestrated a coup of the corrupt and widely disliked Cuban government in 1952. His second rule, however, was more brutal and dictatorial. He manipulated presidential elections, cracked down on newspapers, outlawed strikes, and embezzled money from the state. The economy struggled while Batista's secret police carried out a campaign of repressive terror and torture, killing hundreds and perhaps thousands of people.

Though there is no doubt that Batista was a dictator, there has been considerable controversy about how oppressive his rule was, especially in comparison to the Communist regime that succeeded it. In congressional testimony on the Cuban revolution, former ambassador to Cuba Arthur Gardner argued that Cuba under Fidel Castro was more of a police state than it had been under Batista. He also asserted that Batista was an excellent ally to the United States.

"Batista had always leaned toward the United States. I don't think we ever had a better friend. It was regrettable, like all South Americans, that he was known—although I had no absolute knowledge of it—to be getting a cut, I think is the word for it, in almost all the things that were done. But, on the other hand, he was doing an amazing job. . . ."

In the same testimony, Earl T. Smith, also a former ambassador to Cuba, contended that Batista enjoyed wide support in the armed forces and labor, and that under Batista, "nineteen hundred and fifty-seven was one of the best years in the economic history of Cuba."

These views have been echoed by more modern commentators as well. For example, Adolfo Rivero Caro, a Cuban exile and one of the founders of the Cuban Committee for Human Rights, published an article, *En defensa del neoliberalismo*, in which he argued that on the eve of the revolution, Cuba had a vibrant middle class, as well as life expectancies and average incomes that were well above the average for the region. He admits that the country had many problems, but asks, "Can it truthfully be said that Cuba before Castro was a society without hope and in need of a radical revolution?"

Others, however, have argued that the overthrow of Batista was necessary. During the late 1950s, numerous State Department officials in the United States grew increasingly horrified at Batista's repression and violence. Lyman B. Kirkpatrick, a Central Intelligence Agency officer, said in his 1968 book *The Real CIA*, "By the time Batista fled Havana, he had lost the support of most of the Cuban people as the result of the progressive tyranny and terror he imposed." As an example of this terror, Kirkpatrick recounts the story of a schoolteacher who was arrested and tortured on suspicion of plotting against the government. Kirkpatrick saw photographs of the woman, taken by a doctor who, according to Kirkpatrick, said that "he had never seen a human body more mistreated."

More recent writers have also emphasized the harshness of the Batista regime. In an August 28, 2006, article at the GlobalResearch website, Stephen Lendman argues that the revolution was prompted and necessitated by Batista's rule. He contends, "Batista, with full backing from the US, instituted a brutal police state that served the interests of capital and turned the island into a casino and brothel."

Lendman believes that the Cuban revolution was an effort to remove the corrupt Batista and rid the island of US imperialism. He argues that as such, it was successful, and that the Cuban people were liberated by, and remain grateful for, Castro's revolution.

The authors in *Opposing Viewpoints: Cuba* look at other controversies surrounding Cuba in chapters titled What Is the State of Cuba?, What Is Cuba's Relationship with the World?, What Is the Relationship Between Cuba Policy and US Domestic Politics?, and What Should Be the US Policy Toward Cuba? The viewpoints offer different perspectives on Castro's Cuba and the long legacy of the revolution.

OPPOSING
VIEWPOINTS®
SERIES

CHAPTER 1

What Is the State of Cuba?

Chapter Preface

Internet access in Cuba is among the worst in the world. When Nick Miroff, a contributor to National Public Radio, conducted an unscientific snap poll for a December 14, 2011, article, he found that only two of the twelve Cubans he spoke to had ever been online. Miroff reported that even cyber-cafés did not actually provide cyber access. Instead, they merely allowed users to send and receive e-mail—not to browse the Internet. In a June 28, 2012, article on *Salon*, Miroff added that Cuban government statistics give the island the lowest rate of Internet penetration in the Western Hemisphere.

Various reasons have been advanced for Cuba's failure to provide Internet connections for its people. The government itself has said that the US trade embargo has retarded access. In the *Salon* article, Miroff argued that there is some truth to this. He pointed out, for example, that the Cuban trade embargo blocks Cubans from using a web-traffic analysis tool called Google Analytics.

The United States also has attempted contradictorily to increase Internet access in Cuba in the hope of opening Cuba to democracy and undermining the current Communist regime. Miroff said that this policy may actually result in limiting Cuban access. Miroff argued that "the more US democracy-promotion programs seem aimed at sparking a 'Cuban Spring' on the island, the more Cuban officialdom seems to view the Internet with trepidation." For example, the United States employed Alan Gross as a subcontractor to bring in satellite technology for Internet access to some Cuban communities; the Cuban government labeled this espionage and placed Gross in prison for fifteen years.

Still, the main barrier to access, according to many commentators, is the Cuban government, which wants to restrict outside information and prevent criticism. In a November 18,

2010, article, Guillermo Santamaria reported in the blog *Plu Ultra Technologies/30 Steps* that Cuba "bans private Internet connections." Cubans, he said, therefore have to use Internet services at public computing centers, where "any 'subversive' words that are used in a search will trigger the installed police software."

In an April 23, 2012, article in the *Miami Herald*, Franco Ordonez added that the Internet is actually available for foreign tourists and high-ranking officials. The restrictions, then, are specifically to prevent ordinary Cubans from getting online and expressing dissent or organizing against the government. Ordonez spoke to a twenty-year-old Cuban, David Gonzalez, who said that Internet access is the greatest desire of most young people in Cuba. But, he added, "No one has the Internet. . . . Not the young people. Not the old people. Really the only people who have the Internet are the people with power."

Internet usage in Cuba, then, ties into economic opportunity, Cuban-US relations, and government repression. The authors of the viewpoints in the following chapter look at other aspects of daily life in Cuba as well as the relationship between everyday experiences and national and international issues.

"The time has come to move the Cuban people from wholesale dependence on the state to a new era of individual responsibility and citizenship."

Cuba Is Moving Toward Capitalist Economic Liberalization

Ted Piccone

Ted Piccone is a senior fellow and deputy director of foreign policy at the Brookings Institution. In the following viewpoint, he argues that Raúl Castro's regime in Cuba is instituting important economic changes. Piccone says that the regime is moving cautiously toward more private enterprise, less dependence on the state, and ultimately toward a more vibrant capitalist economy, with more wealth and more inequality. Piccone suggests that the resulting economy will be more like China's or Vietnam's and will encourage more private businesses and more tourism. He concludes that Cuba's changes will eventually lead to normalized relationships with the United States.

As you read, consider the following questions:

1. According to Piccone, what "tough measures" are included in the Cuban economic reforms?

2. What does Piccone say is the risk for Cuba if the pace of change is too slow?

3. What decision by President Barack Obama has affected tourism in Cuba, according to Piccone?

As I sat on the curb in front of central Havana's [El] Capitolio, the impressive domed hall that resembles the U.S. Capitol building, and watched the 1950s-era Plymouths and Soviet-made Ladas go belching by, I was sure I had entered a surreal time warp a mere one-hour flight from Miami. And yet, after a week of meetings with Cuban and foreign diplomats, journalists, academics and artists, I became convinced that Cuba, indeed, is changing in many ways.

An Updating Economy

As a relative newcomer to the intricacies of the Cuba question, I was immediately struck by Cuba's unique blend of decaying splendor, cultural prosperity, restricted freedoms and relative poverty. As everyone knows, Cuba's highly centralized system, with its impressive achievements in health, education and the arts, is still recovering from the loss of massive Soviet subsidies, hurricanes and a steady outflow of its well-educated workforce. Creditors in China and elsewhere are growing tired of underwriting Cuba's struggling economy as it tries to move away from its ossified past and into the 21st century. So something had to be done about liberalizing the economy.

A closer look, however, reveals something more profound—a wholesale mental shift, outlined clearly by President Raúl Castro over the last two years, that the time has come to move the Cuban people from wholesale dependence on the state to a new era of individual responsibility and citizenship.

This is going to take time. The economic reforms or "updating" of Cuba's Soviet-style economic system, approved last spring [2011] at the Communist Party's first National Congress in 14 years, are just beginning to be enacted. They include an expansion of licenses for private enterprise (over 350,000 have been granted), opening more idle land to farmers and cooperatives, allowing businesses to hire employees, empowering people to buy and sell their houses and cars, and opening new lines of credit with no legal ceilings on how much Cubans can borrow. Non-state actors are allowed now to sell unlimited services and commodities directly to state-owned enterprises and joint ventures, thereby opening new channels of commercial activity between farmers and tourist hotels, for example. Think Vietnam or China. The reforms include tough measures too, like shrinking the buying power of the long-standing ration card that every Cuban gets to purchase subsidized basic goods, cutting unemployment benefits, and eventually dismissing anywhere from 500,000 to one million employees from the state sector as bureaucratic middlemen become obsolete and tax revenues rise.

Capitalism Is Coming

These changes, while painful, are reason enough to be optimistic about Cuba's economic future. But something much more fundamental is at work—a turn away from government control of pricing and subsidizing products throughout the economy to a more decentralized framework of subsidizing persons based on need. At heart, the Castro government is prepared to move Cuba from a society based on equity of results to equality of opportunity, infused with a culture of humanism. Not that Cuba's system ever offered true equality, as one taxi driver reminded me as we drove down Havana's famous seaside Malecón. The door, however, is now opening wider to the inevitable rise in inequality that comes from capitalism, even restrained forms of it. Whether one is able to prosper as a self-employed restaurateur, or is the beneficiary of generous relatives sending remittances and goods home from Miami, new gradations in Cuba's economic and social strata are on the way. As long as someone arrives at their

Raúl Castro, President of Cuba

Raúl Castro is, in many respects, an unlikely world leader. Although he became president of Cuba in 2008, he has spent much of his life in the shadow of his older brother, longtime Cuban dictator Fidel Castro. While he has played a key role in governing Cuba for decades, Raúl has remained relatively unknown to people outside of his native country. Indeed, the contrasts between Raúl Castro and his more famous sibling are numerous. While Fidel has been beloved by many Cubans for his charisma and idealism, Raúl is recognized more for his quiet, pensive manner; Fidel is serious and resolute, whereas Raúl is self-deprecating and has a sense of humor. Throughout the Castro regime, Raúl has tended to remain out of the spotlight. . . .

Still, in the eyes of most foreign policy experts, there is no question that Raúl Castro has emerged as a formidable leader in his own right. His effectiveness as a military commander has gone unquestioned since he first took charge of the Cuban army following the 1959 revolution. At the same time, while Fidel Castro has remained doggedly committed to the revolutionary foundations of modern Cuba, Raúl has demonstrated an element of adaptability, a quality that has become more apparent since the dissolution of the Soviet Union in the early 1990s. Long considered to be more devoted to Communist ideology than his brother, Raúl has also shown himself to be more flexible and pragmatic than Fidel, particularly in relation to economic policy. Since becoming Cuban president, Raúl Castro has found himself in a new position, forced to reconcile his past ideals with the political and economic demands of the twenty-first century.

"Raúl Castro," Newsmakers: The People Behind Today's Headlines. *Detroit, MI: Gale, 2010.*

wealth legally and pays their taxes, assured one senior party official, they are free to become rich.

The big question for Cuba's leaders today is whether they can bring their people with them down this new, uncertain path after five decades of Cuban-style communism. If reforms happen too quickly, it could cause excessive dislocation and unhappiness and potentially destabilize the regime. Already, bureaucrats who have something to lose under the new system are resisting change, much to Raúl Castro's chagrin. If the pace of change is too slow, on the other hand, budding entrepreneurs, the middle class and disaffected youth, who have no overt commitment to the values of the 1959 revolution, may give up sooner and head to greener pastures in the United States, Spain or Canada. As it is, Cubans are leaving the island in droves to join their families in Florida and beyond, beneficiaries of U.S. policies that grant Cubans preferred immigration benefits once their feet reach American soil, and of Spanish laws that grant some Cubans Spanish citizenship.

The trick for party officials, then, is to demonstrate enough tangible improvements that Cubans will maintain faith in their ability to lead the country even after the Castros leave the scene. This explains the Communist Party's determined effort to intensify popular consultations throughout the island and to keep up the momentum and rhetoric of slow but steady change. "In everything we do," said one official, "we will try to be inclusive."

There is, indeed, a daunting list of challenges ahead. Cuban officials are working overtime to update legal codes and systems to conform to the new economic policies. A revised tax code is being drafted as well as designs for a new labor system that will handle the growing category of self-employed workers not currently covered by Cuba's labor code. A massive education campaign is needed not only to inform and consult the general public but to explain to local officials and civil servants how this is all going to work. New rules for foreign investment remain unfinished business. And major investment is needed to update Cuba's sagging infrastructure, especially in the telecommunications sector where cell phones and Internet penetration remain the lowest in the hemisphere.

Tourism

One area where Cuba seems to be moving in a positive direction is tourism. From 1990 to 2010, the estimated number of tourists has risen from 360,000 to 2.66 million. In addition, thanks to President [Barack] Obama's decision to allow Cuban-American families to visit the island and send remittances as much as they want, Cubans have received over 400,000 visits and roughly $2 billion from relatives in the United States. These are proving to be important sources of currency and commerce that are helping families cope with reduced subsidies and breathe life in the burgeoning private sector. A walk through crowded Old Havana, where construction crews are busy restoring one of the Americas' great colonial treasures, offers compelling evidence that Cuba can be a strong magnet for Europeans, Canadians, Chinese and—some day—hundreds of thousands of American visitors. And Pope Benedict's visit in late March [2012] will shine an international spotlight on a Cuba slowly opening its doors to the world, yes, but more importantly, to an increasingly vocal and confident Catholic Church intent on securing a more prominent and relevant place in Cuban society.

For now, Cuba's slow-motion evolution toward a hybrid phase of economic liberalization and political control remains a work in progress. The next Communist Party conference to be held later this month [January 2012] is likely to bring only modest changes in the regime's aging leadership, for example, but promises of adopting term limits for senior government officials appear all but certain to be fulfilled. Raúl Castro, a military man who believes in discipline, organization and institutions, has instituted regular cabinet meetings and clear lines of communication. In this sense, he is no Fidel [referring to Fidel Castro, former president of Cuba and brother of Raúl Castro]. These, too, are signs of change that will, with time, make long overdue reconciliation with the United States inevitable.

> *"I was elected to defend, maintain and continue perfecting socialism, not to destroy it."*

Cuba Is Moving Toward a More Flexible Socialism, Not Toward Capitalism

Marce Cameron

Marce Cameron is an Australian writer whose work has appeared in Green Left Weekly *and* Direct Action. *In the following viewpoint, he says that Cuban president Raúl Castro is not moving the country toward capitalism. Rather, he says, Castro is reforming the economy to preserve and extend socialism. According to Cameron, Castro is making Cuba's economy more equitable by allowing those who work harder to make more money. Castro is also instituting agricultural reform, so that more private farmers can raise crops by leasing state land. Cameron says that such changes are not just imposed by the government but are being pushed by the Cuban people and workers.*

As you read, consider the following questions:

1. According to Cameron, who is Luis Sexto?

2. Why is egalitarianism a form of exploitation, according to Raúl Castro?

3. What is the *marabu* bush, and how has it affected Cuban agriculture?

Since becoming Cuba's president (initially acting president) in August 2007, when Fidel Castro became gravely ill and had to step down, Raúl Castro has called for a nationwide debate on the future of Cuba's socialist revolution. The debate is aimed at consensus on what must be done to revitalise Cuba's socialist project.

The Revolution Will Not Surrender

Most if not all of the central leadership of the Cuban Communist Party (PCC), led by Fidel and Raúl, who are first and second secretaries respectively, recognise that a radical renovation of Cuba's socialist project is needed if the revolution is to endure in the post-Fidel era. While the debate has unfolded, Cuba has been changing. So far these changes lack the coherence and depth to carry through the necessary and urgent renovation without abandoning the revolution's ethical and political principles.

Yet the direction of the changes, which flow not only from government decrees but from the massive participation of Cuba's working people in critical reflection and debate, is clear enough. To the disappointment of the revolution's enemies abroad, who had hoped that Raúl might lead Cuba towards a restoration of capitalism, Cuba is changing in the spirit of Raúl Castro's response to US demands for US-style "democracy" and capitalist restoration in a speech to Cuba's National Assembly of People's Power on August 1: "[The National Assembly] didn't elect me president to restore capitalism in Cuba or to surrender the Revolution. I was elected to defend, maintain and continue perfecting socialism, not to destroy it."

Respected Cuban journalist Luis Sexto, recipient of the 2009 José Marti journalism award, Cuba's most prestigious, commented on the pro-revolution *Progreso Weekly* website on July 15 [2009]: "Cuban society, rigid for many years, shakes off the starch that immobilized it . . . to change what is obsolete without compromising the solidity of the revolution's power." What's obsolete are many of the revolution's concepts, structures, methods and mentalities.

Economic Reforms

Much of what is obsolete flows from, or is reinforced by, a structural dysfunction in Cuba's post-capitalist, centrally planned economy: While many goods and services are free or heavily subsidised by the socialist state, wages are both insufficient to meet all basic needs and too low to act as much of a stimulus to productivity. In any society, labour productivity growth is the wellspring of economic and social progress.

By reinforcing social inequality that is not linked to the individual's or work collectives' labour contribution to society, excessive universal subsidies, combined with low wages, undermine the economic and ethical foundations of Cuba's socialist project. "Socialism means social justice and equality, but equality of rights, of opportunities, not of income", Raúl said in a speech to the National Assembly on July 11, 2008. "Equality is not the same as egalitarianism. Egalitarianism is in itself a form of exploitation: exploitation of the good workers by those who are less productive and lazy."

A degree of social inequality is inevitable in any post-capitalist society that is not fully Communist. Cuba, a small third world country suffering half a century of US economic siege, is far from a Communist society, which is conceivable only on a world scale. While unavoidable, inequality should be the result of those contributing more to society through their work receiving more from society in the form of goods and services. Yet in Cuba today, people who receive substantial remittances from relatives in wealthy countries such as the US, and those who choose not to work because they're too busy selling goods stolen from the state on the black market, receive the same highly subsidised food rations, among other subsidies, as conscientious and productive workers. In effect, Cuba's working people are subsidising what Fidel called "the new rich".

In a landmark speech at Havana University on November 17, 2005, Fidel warned that the revolution could destroy itself as a result of its own errors and weaknesses, and called for the dismantling of the edifice of universal state subsidies and gratuities—apart from those guaranteed in Cuba's socialist constitution, such as the right to free health care and education—in order to reassert the socialist principle of "to each according to their work". He also called for more public criticism and debate within the revolution to expose official corruption and negligence.

While the structural dysfunction in Cuba's post-capitalist economy has its roots in the malign influence of Soviet bureaucratic "socialism" during the 1970s and '80s, egalitarian paternalism is largely a consequence of emergency measures adopted at the beginning of the Special Period [in Time of Peace], the deep economic crisis precipitated by the demise of the Soviet Union, Cuba's main trading partner, at the beginning of the 1990s. Cuba is yet to fully recover from this crisis period, but oil-rich Venezuela, now undergoing its own socialist revolution, brings Cuba some much-needed moral and material reinforcement. The convergent paths and growing integration of these two revolutions add impetus to the socialist renovation that has begun in Cuba.

Among the economic reforms initiated under Raúl's presidency, the cap on bonus payments tied to productivity has been lifted, and a new payments system that ties incomes to productivity is being generalised across state enterprises; Cubans may now hold multiple jobs and students may work part-time to supplement their allowances and gain work experience; and excessive universal subsides are being gradually withdrawn. The aim of these reforms is to put more money in the pockets of productive workers, allowing more workers and their dependants to live with dignity on their legal incomes, rather than having to turn to the black market to make ends meet.

"From now on, if the bureaucracy doesn't hold us back . . . [n]obody will have to wait for the generous hand of the state for an increase in salary or pension, which may have to be postponed. . . . If you need it, or if you want to live more comfortably, you can work more," Luis Sexto commented on July 15.

In other reforms, Cubans may now stay in tourist hotels and buy electrical goods such as mobile phones, computers and electric scooters. Previously, Cubans other than hotel workers were barred from entering tourist hotels in an effort to contain the negative social consequences of Cuba's opening to foreign tourism, such as prostitution. The sale of consumer electronics was limited to discourage visible displays of social inequality in times of great hardship, which would undermine social solidarity, and to prevent the collapse of Cuba's antiquated electrical grid prior to the "energy revolution" launched in 2005. Now that workers and farmers can legitimately earn higher incomes, they have to be able to spend this money on something.

Agricultural Reforms

The most significant reforms so far have been in agriculture. Raúl has declared increasing food production the government's top priority and a matter of national security. While Cuba spends billions of dollars on food imports, half the farmland has been lying idle, much of it overrun with a woody tropical weed known as the *marabu* bush. The government is promot-

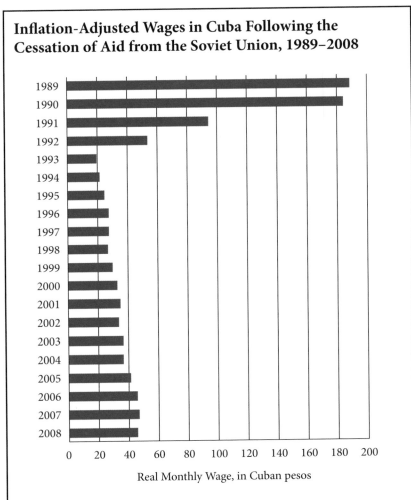

Inflation-Adjusted Wages in Cuba Following the Cessation of Aid from the Soviet Union, 1989–2008

Real Monthly Wage, in Cuban pesos

TAKEN FROM: Arch Ritter, "Has Cuba's Catastrophic Decline in Real Wage Levels Been Reversed?," *The Cuban Economy* (blog), June 22, 2010. http://thecubaneconomy.com.

ing a large-scale "return to the land". In Cuba, most arable land is socially owned, while some belongs to peasant farmers.

Land belonging to the state will not be privatised. Rather, individuals, cooperatives and state farms are being encouraged to grow crops or raise livestock on idle state land. Raúl reported to the National Assembly in December that 54% of this land, or almost a million hectares, had been granted in usufruct, i.e., leased rent-free on a long-term basis. These land grants have benefited around 100,000 people. A social movement among producers has sprung up to pass on knowledge to new farmers. Urban agriculture, the outstanding success story of Cuba's large-scale transition to more sustainable farming methods during the past two decades, is being complemented by creating or consolidating "green belts" around the cities.

Farmers can now buy some supplies directly from a new chain of state stores instead of everything being centrally allocated by the state, while the state has greatly increased what it pays to producers to stimulate production and thus lower prices in the free markets. Guaranteeing a stable supply of cheap locally produced food to replace expensive imports is a precondition for the elimination of the *libreta*, or ration book, through which all Cubans are guaranteed a monthly quota of highly subsidized food and other basic goods.

In a bold administrative decentralisation, responsibility for deciding what crops and livestock are to be farmed where has been devolved from the agriculture ministry in Havana and the provincial capitals to Cuba's 169 municipalities, bypassing a notorious chain of administrative bottlenecks. In November, a report in the newspaper *Granma* estimated an excess of 89,000 administrative personnel, some 26% of the total, in the state farm sector alone. This "engenders bureaucracy, raises costs, hampers productivity, creates disorder and prevents workers from improving their incomes". A rationalisation and reorganisation of the sector, long plagued by inefficiency, has begun. In March [2010], the government announced that around 100 unproductive state farms would be closed.

From Above and Below

To sum up the changes under Raúl's presidency, they are broadly consistent with the diagnosis made by Fidel in his

November 17, 2005, speech at Havana University and the line of march he proposed then to achieve "true and irreversible socialism", while not being limited to the ideas expressed by Fidel then or since.

Secondly, while most of these changes flow from government decrees, some—such as efforts to forge a more mature and permanent culture of public criticism and debate within the revolution, and the gains won against homophobia in recent years—result from encouragement or support "from above" meeting with a groundswell of activism "from below" to overcome administrative opposition, inertia and backward attitudes.

Thirdly, the pace of change is constrained by the need to strive for consensus on the most far-reaching changes and the fact that the Cuban leadership has had to devote much of its energies to crisis management, because of the devastating 2008 hurricanes—which caused economic losses equivalent to a fifth of Cuba's GDP [gross domestic product], and from which the country is still recovering—and the global economic turmoil of the past year and a half [stemming from the worldwide financial crisis of 2007–2012], which has hit the Cuban economy hard. This makes further changes all the more urgent, yet it has also delayed their timely implementation. The Sixth PCC Congress, originally scheduled for late 2009, has been postponed at least a year, and a new date has yet to be publicly announced. On the plus side, this leaves more time for a clarifying public debate and the PCC's internal preparations for the congress.

As Luis Sexto noted in a March 24 commentary for *Progreso Weekly*, "A careful observer might even believe that the revolutionary government (well described, because of the renovative task it has to perform) is subjected to intense pressure from its bases of support." Here Sexto is referring to the popular mood for changes in the direction of socialist renovation. Yet administrative opposition and inertia have proven to be formidable obstacles to the implementation of reforms decreed by the government, while among those who urge a socialist renovation there is a vigorous debate. Thus, "We perceive a tug ... about what to change and how much to change without excessively endangering the power achieved by the Revolution and sometimes, unfortunately, the bureaucratic power of some entrepreneurial entities", Sexto observed.

Progreso Weekly's Havana bureau editor Manuel Alberto Ramy commented on March 31: "We are burdened by a government apparatus that is overweight, excessively centralized and plagued with bureaucrats who turn their little parcels of power into knightly feuds. And many of them, instead of adequately enforcing the decisions [of the revolutionary government], have an infinite capacity for hindering, delaying and/or sidetracking them." Following the announcement of the closure of 100 inefficient state farms and the redeployment of their 40,000 workers to more productive work, Manuel Alberto Ramy hears of "similar stirrings in other ministries and institutions" that have "begun to study the convenience of turning some of [their] companies into cooperative societies". Such studies indicate that widening the scope of cooperative forms of ownership or management of certain productive entities has "received the blessing of the political leadership of this country", and suggests that "the top circles of leadership have sketched a more flexible economic model and are willing to explore it gradually and assume the consequences."

"Dissenters are punished daily in nearly every aspect of their lives."

Cuba Continues to Violate Human Rights

Human Rights Watch

Human Rights Watch (HRW) is a nongovernmental organization that researches and advocates for human rights worldwide. In the following viewpoint, HRW reports that new Cuban president Raúl Castro has continued the Cuban government's policy of repression and human rights abuse. HRW says that dissidents in Cuba who criticize the government are subject to harassment, ostracism, and imprisonment in brutal conditions. HRW says that international efforts by the United States, Canada, Europe, and Latin American nations have been ineffectual and have not improved Cuba's human rights record. HRW recommends a concerted international effort aimed at the single goal of pressuring the Cuban government to release political prisoners.

As you read, consider the following questions:

1. According to HRW, what is the "dangerousness" provision in Cuban law, and how is it used by the state?

2. Why does HRW say that it was difficult to gather information about Cuba, and how did it research its report?

3. Why does HRW say that the American embargo on Cuba has been a failure?

In July 2006, Fidel Castro handed control of the Cuban government over to his brother Raúl Castro. As the new head of state, Raúl Castro inherited a system of abusive laws and institutions, as well as responsibility for hundreds of political prisoners arrested during his brother's rule. Rather than dismantle this repressive machinery, Raúl Castro has kept it firmly in place and fully active. Scores of political prisoners arrested under Fidel Castro continue to languish in Cuba's prisons. And Raúl Castro's government has used draconian laws and sham trials to incarcerate scores more who have dared to exercise their fundamental freedoms.

Imprisoned for "Dangerousness"

Raúl Castro's government has relied in particular on a provision of the Cuban criminal code that allows the state to imprison individuals before they have committed a crime, on the suspicion that they might commit an offense in the future. This "dangerousness" provision is overtly political, defining as "dangerous" any behavior that contradicts socialist norms. The most Orwellian [that is, reminiscent of the repressive dystopian state in George Orwell's novel *1984*] of Cuba's laws, it captures the essence of the Cuban government's repressive mind-set, which views anyone who acts out of step with the government as a potential threat and thus worthy of punishment.

Despite significant obstacles to research, Human Rights Watch documented more than 40 cases in which Cuba has imprisoned individuals for "dangerousness" under Raúl Castro because they tried to exercise their fundamental rights. We believe there are many more. The "dangerous" activities in these cases have included handing out copies of the Universal Declaration of Human Rights, staging peaceful marches, writing news articles critical of the government, and attempting to organize independent unions.

The Raúl Castro government has applied the "dangerousness" law not only to dissenters and critics of the government, but to a broad range of people who choose not to cooperate with the state. We found that failing to attend pro-government rallies, not belonging to official party organizations, and being unemployed are all considered signs of "antisocial" behavior, and may lead to "official warnings" and even incarceration in Raúl Castro's Cuba. In a January 2009 campaign called "Operation Victory," dozens of individuals in eastern Cuba—most of them youth—were charged with "dangerousness" for being unemployed. So was a man from Sancti Spíritus who could not work because of health problems, and was sentenced to two years' imprisonment in August 2008 for being unemployed.

In addition to "dangerousness," Cuba has a wide range of other laws that criminalize the exercise of fundamental freedoms, including laws penalizing contempt, insubordination, and acts against the independence of the state. Indeed, article 62 of the Cuban constitution prohibits the exercise of any basic right that runs contrary to "the ends of the socialist state." Together with a judicial system that lacks independence and systematically violates due process rights, Raúl Castro's government has employed such laws to imprison scores of peaceful dissidents.

Dissent and Repression

Imprisonment is only one of the many tactics the Cuban government uses to repress fundamental freedoms. Dissidents who try to express their views are often beaten, arbitrarily arrested, and subjected to public acts of repudiation. The government monitors, intimidates, and threatens those it perceives as its enemies. It isolates them from their friends and neighbors and discriminates against their families.

Cuba attempts to justify this repression as a legitimate response to a US policy aimed at toppling the Castro government. It is true that the United States has a long history of intervention on the island, and its current policy explicitly aims to support a change in Cuba's government. However, in the scores of cases Human Rights Watch examined for this [viewpoint], this argument falls flat.

The reason that human rights advocate Ramón Velásquez Toranzo set out on a peaceful march across Cuba and journalist Raymundo Perdigón Brito wrote articles critical of the Castro government was not because they were agents of the US government, but rather because they saw problems with their own. Yet because these dissidents expressed their opinions openly, both were imprisoned by Raúl Castro's government, like scores of others. Rather than being a legitimate defense against a threat to national security, these and other cases reveal a state that uses repression to enforce conformity with its political agenda.

It is important to note that the term "dissidents" in the Cuban context does not refer to a homogenous group of people who share a single ideology, affiliation, or common objective. Rather, it refers to anyone who—like Velásquez and Perdigón—engages in activities the government deems contrary to its political agenda. Some dissidents may advocate for democratic change or reform of the socialist system from within; while others may be apolitical, focusing instead on a single issue such as the right to practice their religion or organize a trade union.

Dissidents are a small and significantly isolated segment of the population. However, their marginalization is evidence not of the lack of dissent in Cuba, but rather of the state's ruthless efficiency in suppressing it. Fear permeates all aspects of dissidents' lives. Some stop voicing their opinions and abandon their activities altogether; others continue to exercise their rights, but live in constant dread of being punished. Many more never express dissent to avoid reprisals. As human rights defender Rodolfo Barthelemy Coba told Human Rights Watch in March 2009, "We live 24 hours a day ready to be detained." Ten days after making that statement, Barthelemy was arrested and taken to prison without trial, where he remains today.

While this [viewpoint] documents a systematic pattern of repression, it does not intend to suggest that there are no outlets for dissent whatsoever in Cuba. The last three years have, for example, witnessed the emergence of an independent Cuban blogosphere, critical lyrics by musicians, and most recently a series of government-organized public meetings to reflect on Cuban socialism.

Upon closer examination, however, these examples show just how circumscribed spaces of dissent are and, as a result, how incredibly limited their impact is on society on the whole. While some bloggers speak to problems in Cuba, they must publish their work through back channels—saving documents on memory sticks and uploading entries through illegal connections. Because an hour of Internet use costs one-third of Cubans' monthly wages and is available exclusively in a few government-run centers, only a tiny fraction of Cubans have the chance to read such blogs—including, ironically, bloggers themselves. Some bands perform lyrics that criticize the government, but their songs are banned from the airwaves, their performances shut down, and their members harassed and arbitrarily detained. And while it is true that Raúl Castro's government organized meetings recently to reflect on Cuban socialism, the agenda for these discussions explicitly prohibited any talk of reforming the single-party system.

Cuba has made important advances in the progressive realization of some economic, social, and cultural rights such as education and health care. For example, UNESCO [United Nations Educational, Scientific and Cultural Organization] has concluded that there is near-universal literacy on the island and UNICEF [United Nations Children's Fund] has projected that the country is on track to achieve most of the Millennium Development Goals. However, the stark reality is that this progress has not been matched in respect for civil and political rights.

The Raúl Castro government has at times signaled a willingness to reconsider its long-standing disregard for human rights norms. In February 2008, Cuba signed the International Covenant on Civil and Political Rights (ICCPR) and the International Covenant on Economic, Social and Cultural Rights (ICESCR), and commuted the death sentences of all prisoners except for three individuals charged with terrorism. Yet the Castro government has yet to ratify the ICCPR and ICESCR, and continues to flout many of the treaties' core principles. And Cuban law still allows individuals who undermine the independence of the state to be sentenced to death.

The Cuban government has for years refused to recognize the legitimacy of independent human rights monitoring and has adamantly refused to allow international monitors, such as the International Committee of the Red Cross and international nongovernmental organizations like Human Rights Watch, to visit the island and investigate human rights conditions. In researching this [viewpoint], Human Rights Watch made repeated written requests to the Raúl Castro government for meetings with authorities and formal authorization to conduct a fact-finding mission to the island. As in the past, the Cuban government did not respond to any of our requests.

As a result, Human Rights Watch decided to conduct a fact-finding mission to Cuba without official permission in June and July 2009. During this trip, Human Rights Watch researchers conducted extensive interviews in seven of the island's fourteen provinces. We also conducted numerous interviews via telephone from New York City. In total, we carried out more than 60 in-depth interviews with human rights defenders, journalists, former political prisoners, family members of current political prisoners, members of the clergy, trade unionists, and other Cuban citizens.

Those interviews, together with extensive research from January to November 2009, are the basis of the following findings.

The Legal Foundation of Repression in Cuba

Cuba's laws empower the state to criminalize virtually all forms of dissent. Article 62 of the Cuban constitution explicitly prohibits Cubans from exercising their basic rights against the "ends of the socialist state." Cubans who dare to criticize the government are subject to draconian criminal and "pre-criminal" charges, such as "dangerousness." They are exempted from due process guarantees. They are denied meaningful judicial protection. And they are left without recourse to international human rights mechanisms.

> A person is considered to be in a state of dangerousness due to antisocial behavior if the person ... lives, like a social parasite, off the work of others.
>
> —Article 73 of the Criminal Code, on one kind of "antisocial behavior" that constitutes "dangerousness."

Political Prisoners and Due Process Violations

Raúl Castro's government has imprisoned scores of political prisoners using laws criminalizing dissent. In particular, Cuba has relied on a "dangerousness" provision that allows authorities to imprison individuals for exercising their fundamental freedoms, on the grounds that their activities contradict "socialist morality." The provision has more broadly been applied to non-dissident Cubans who choose not to work for the gov-

Dissidents in Cuba

A human rights group known as the Ladies in White (*Damas de Blanco*) was formed in April 2003 by the wives, mothers, daughters, sisters, and aunts of the members of the "group of 75" dissidents arrested a month earlier in Cuba's human rights crackdown. The group conducts peaceful protests calling for the unconditional release of political prisoners.... In April 2008, 10 members of the Ladies in White were physically removed from a park near the Plaza of the Revolution in Havana when they demanded the release of their husbands and the other members of the "group of 75" still imprisoned. The group held protests during the third week of March 2010 to commemorate the March 2003 crackdown. Cuban security forces and government-orchestrated mobs forcefully broke up the protests on March 16 and 17.... Through the intercession of Roman Catholic Cardinal Jaime Ortega [y Alamino], the Cuban government ended the harassment in early May 2010 and allowed the Ladies in White to continue with their weekly marches.

Cuban Internet blogger Yoani Sánchez has received considerable international attention since late 2007 for her website, Generación Y, which includes commentary critical of the Cuban government.... On November 6, 2009, Sánchez and two other bloggers, Orlando Luis Pardo and Claudia Cadelo, were intercepted by state security agents while walking on a Havana street on their way to participate in a march against violence. Sánchez and Pardo were beaten in the assault. The US Department of State issued a statement deploring the assault and expressed its deep concern to the Cuban government for the incident.

Mark P. Sullivan, Cuba: Issues For the 112th Congress, *Congressional Research Service, July 20, 2012.*

ernment, and are thus viewed as a threat. Meanwhile, Raúl Castro continues to imprison scores of dissidents unjustly sentenced for exercising their fundamental freedoms under Fidel Castro, including 53 human rights defenders, journalists, civil society leaders, and other dissenters arrested in a massive 2003 crackdown. . . .

Cuba systematically violates the due process rights of dissenters from the moment they are arrested through their sham trials. Political detainees are routinely denied access to legal counsel and family visits, held in inhumane and dangerous conditions, and subjected to forced interrogations. Neither detainees nor their families are adequately informed about the charges against them, and political detainees may be held for months or years without ever being formally tried for a crime. Nearly all trials of political detainees are closed hearings lasting less than one hour, during which dissidents are subjected to politically motivated rulings and even falsification of evidence by security officials and prosecutors. Human Rights Watch was unable to document a single case under the Raúl Castro government where a court acquitted a political detainee. . . .

Cuba's prison officials, like the Cuban government as a whole, punish dissent. Conditions for political prisoners and common prisoners alike are overcrowded, unhygienic, and unhealthy, leading to extensive malnutrition and illness. Political prisoners who criticize the government, refuse to participate in ideological "re-education," or engage in hunger strikes or other forms of protest are routinely subjected to extended solitary confinement, beatings, restrictions of visits, and the denial of medical care. Prisoners have no effective complaint mechanism to seek redress, granting prison authorities total impunity. Taken together, these forms of cruel, inhuman, and degrading treatment may rise to the level of torture.

> The cells are one meter or one-and-a-half meters wide by
> two meters long. You sleep during the day on a concrete

platform and at night you get a mattress, which is removed at daybreak. You are not allowed to have any belongings, and the food is terrible. . . . Some cells have a little window, others none. Some cells have light, others don't.

—Victor Yunier Fernández Martínez describes the conditions in solitary confinement, where he was sent repeatedly during his imprisonment for "dangerousness" from 2006 to 2009. Fernández, a political activist, was incarcerated in the prisons of Canaleta and 1580.

Everyday Forms of Repression

Dissenters are punished daily in nearly every aspect of their lives. The Cuban government routinely uses short-term arrests to harass dissidents or prevent them from participating in groups or activities considered "counterrevolutionary." Dissidents are beaten, publicly humiliated, and threatened by security officers and groups of civilians tied to the state. They are denied work, fired from jobs, and fined, placing significant financial strain on their families. They are prevented from exercising their right to travel within and outside of the island. And they are subjected to invasive surveillance, which violates their privacy and gathers information that can later be used to imprison them. These tactics of repression are consistently visited on the families of dissenters as well. . . .

Cuba's systematic repression has created a pervasive climate of fear among dissidents and when it comes to expression of political views in Cuban society as a whole. This climate hinders the exercise of basic rights, pressuring Cubans to show their allegiance to the state, while discouraging any form of criticism. Dissidents feel as though they are constantly being watched—a sense that fosters distrust among peers and self-censorship. They fear they will be arrested at any moment, and have no confidence in the willingness of the government to protect their rights or give them a fair trial. This climate of fear has led to the near-complete isolation of dissidents from their communities, friends, and sometimes even families, which together with other forms of repression has had profound emotional consequences, including depression and signs of trauma. . . .

International Responses to Cuban Rights Abuses

Given the effectiveness of Cuba's repressive machinery and the Castro government's firm grip on power, the pressure needed to bring progress on human rights cannot come solely from within Cuba. In order to succeed, it must be supported by effective pressure on the part of the international community. Currently, this effective pressure—whether from Latin American countries, the United States, Canada, or Europe—is lacking.

Efforts by the US government to press for change by imposing a sweeping economic embargo have proven to be a costly and misguided failure. The embargo imposes indiscriminate hardship on the Cuban population as a whole, and has done nothing to improve the situation of human rights in Cuba. Rather than isolating Cuba, the policy has isolated the United States, enabling the Castro government to garner sympathy abroad while simultaneously alienating Washington's potential allies.

There is no question: The Cuban government bears full and exclusive responsibility for the abuses it commits. However, so long as the embargo remains in place, the Castro government will continue to manipulate US policy to cast itself as a Latin American David standing up to the US Goliath, a role it exploits skillfully.

Just as the US embargo policy has proved counterproductive, so have the policies of the European Union [EU] and Canada failed to exert effective pressure on Cuba. The EU's Common Position sets clear human rights benchmarks for economic cooperation with Cuba, but the cost of noncompliance has been insufficient to compel change by the Castro government. Canada lacks such benchmarks, promoting significant investment in the island at the same time as it decries the Cuban government's abuses.

Worse still, Latin American governments across the political spectrum have been reluctant to criticize Cuba, and in some cases have openly embraced the Castro government, despite its dismal human rights record. Countries like Venezuela, Bolivia, and Ecuador hold Cuba up as a model, while others quietly admit its abuses even as they enthusiastically push for Cuba's reintegration into regional bodies such as the Organization of American States (OAS). The silence of the Latin governments condones Cuba's abusive behavior and perpetuates a climate of impunity that allows repression to continue. This is particularly troubling coming from a region in which many countries have learned firsthand the high cost of international indifference to state-sponsored repression.

Not only have all of these policies—US, European, Canadian, and Latin American—failed individually to improve human rights in Cuba, but their divided and even contradictory nature has allowed the Cuban government to evade effective pressure and deflect criticism of its practices.

To remedy this continuing failure, the US must end its failed embargo policy. It should shift the goal of its Cuba strategy away from regime change and toward promoting human rights. In particular, it should replace its sweeping bans on travel and trade with Cuba with more effective forms of pressure.

This move would fundamentally shift the balance in the Cuban government's relationship with its own people and the international community. No longer would Cuba be able to manipulate the embargo as a pretext for repressing its own people. Nor would other countries be able to blame the US policy for their own failures to hold Cuba accountable for its abuses.

Release All Political Prisoners

However, ending the current embargo policy by itself will not bring an end to Cuba's repression. Only a multilateral approach will have the political power and moral authority to press the Cuban government to end its repressive practices. Therefore, before changing its policy, the US should work to secure commitments from the EU, Canada, and Latin American allies that they will join together to pressure Cuba to meet a single, concrete demand: the immediate and unconditional release of all political prisoners.

In order to enforce this demand, the multilateral coalition should establish a clear definition of who constitutes a political prisoner—one that includes all Cubans imprisoned for exercising their fundamental rights, including those incarcerated for the pre-criminal offense of "dangerousness" and the 53 dissidents still in prison from the 2003 crackdown. It should also set a firm deadline for compliance, granting the Raúl Castro government six months to meet this demand.

Most important, the members of the coalition should commit themselves to holding the Cuban government accountable should it fail to release its political prisoners. The penalties should be significant enough that they bear real consequences for the Cuban government. And they should be focused enough to target the Cuban leadership, rather than the Cuban population on the whole. Options include adopting targeted sanctions on the government officials, such as travel bans and asset freezes, and withholding any new forms of foreign investment until Cuba meets the demand.

During the six-month period, Latin American countries, Canada, the EU, and the US should be able to choose individually whether or not to impose their own restrictions on Cuba. Some may enact targeted sanctions on Cuba's leadership immediately, while others may put no restrictions on Cuba during that time.

Regardless, if the Castro government is still holding political prisoners at the end of six months, Cuba must be held accountable. All of the countries must honor their agreement and impose joint punitive measures on Cuba that will effectively pressure the Castro government to release its political prisoners.

On the other hand, if the Cuban government releases all political prisoners—whether before or after the six-month period is complete—these punitive measures should be lifted. Then, the multilateral coalition should devise a sustained, incremental strategy to push the Raúl Castro government to improve its human rights record. This strategy should focus on pressuring Cuba to reform its laws criminalizing dissent, dismantle the repressive institutions that enforce them, and end abuses of basic rights. And the impact of the strategy should be monitored regularly to ensure it is not creating more repression than it curbs.

Ultimately, it is the Raúl Castro government that bears responsibility for such abuses—and has the power to address them. Yet as the last three years of Raúl Castro's rule show, Cuba will not improve its human rights record unless it is pressured to do so.

| "The reason it is possible to sustain the health and education levels is simple: political will."

Cuba's Government Works to Advance Health and Education

Jonathan Glennie

Jonathan Glennie is a research fellow in Centre for Aid and Public Expenditure (CAPE) at the Overseas Development Institute (ODI), and he is the author of The Trouble with Aid: Why Less Could Mean More for Africa. *In the following viewpoint, he argues that, despite human rights abuses and political repression, Cuba has made excellent progress in areas such as health care and education. Glennie notes that this progress has been made despite a weak economy. Glennie suggests that the progress is due to the government's political commitment to social services. He concludes that, in this respect, other nations should emulate Cuba.*

As you read, consider the following questions:

1. What regional governments does Glennie say are making good progress toward the UN Millennium Development Goals (MDGs)?

2. Where does Glennie say the MDG Report Card placed Cuba in relation to other countries worldwide in meeting the Millennium Development Goals?

3. What does Glennie's Cuban economist friend say Cuba does to keep health and education of high quality in the country?

As we discuss how well countries are progressing on the [United Nations] Millennium Development Goals (MDGs), South America's left-leaning governments are coming out of it all quite well. And while their mix of policies more closely resembles modified liberal capitalism than revolutionary socialism (yes, even under the radical governments of [Venezuela's Hugo] Chávez, [Bolivia's Evo] Morales and [Ecuador's Rafael] Correa), it is to Cuba that most still look for political inspiration. Ask Luiz Inácio Lula da Silva, the moderate social democratic president of Brazil and the world's latest favourite leader, for his political heroes, and I bet [longtime Cuban leader Fidel] Castro will be in the top three.

Cuba and the MDGs

So it is worth looking at how Cuba itself is doing on the MDGs. Of course, the very fact that I am mentioning the C-word will produce harangues from some quarters that I am a Marxist-Leninist apologist who turns a blind eye to human rights abuses. I am not, and I don't. But the evidence suggests that Cuba has made excellent progress towards the MDGs in the last decade, building on what are already universally acknowledged to be outstanding achievements in equitable health and education standards. So it is important for researchers to check the figures and reflect on the reasons for them, just as we do with other countries in the world, and without denying the serious political and economic problems in the country.

According to a new MDG Report Card by the Overseas Development Institute, Cuba is among the 20 best-performing countries in the world. The key question for development experts who want to learn from this success is this: How is progress being made when the economy appears to be in such turmoil? I posed this question to a young Cuban economist friend of mine and his answer is worth reflecting on (I will let the fact that he doesn't want his name to appear, despite saying positive things about the government, speak for itself regarding freedom of expression):

Hello Jonathan. How is it possible to sustain spending despite economic difficulties? Good question!

The Cuban economy is planned and we redistribute income from the most dynamic sectors, which generate most foreign exchange, towards those that are less dynamic but necessary for the country. That's how we maintain a budget to keep health and education high quality and free of charge to the user.

Although many see this as "social spending", some economists, of which I am one, see it as a long-term (if costly) investment. It is part of the country's economic strategy in the long run to have human capital which can easily adapt to new economic conditions, including the development of trade in services. So costly investments are made, and wages in these sectors are kept relatively high. Since 2004 Cuba has indeed increased exports of services in precisely these sectors (health and education), mainly to Latin countries.

You ask why health and education levels do not match the country's economic development, and that's exactly where the paradox lies. There are some economists, of which I am not one, that think that if more resources were devoted to productive areas, the national economic outlook would improve, and who therefore call for forms of cost recovery. Given the current economic crisis, it has been necessary to

Cuba Has Reduced Its Proportion of Underweight Children

The chart shows the reduction in the percentage of children under the age of five who are underweight.

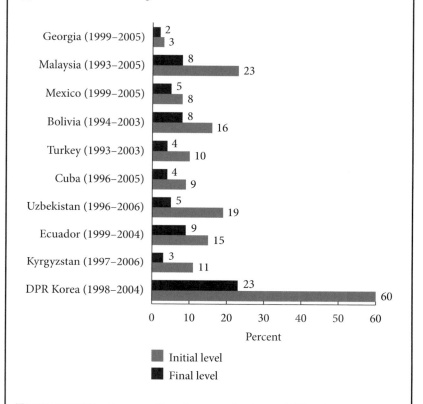

TAKEN FROM: Overseas Development Institute, *Millennium Development Goals (MDG) Report Card: Measuring Progress Across Countries*, 2010, p. 22.

review subsidies, e.g., a small percentage decrease in social assistance, which was very generous. But only in order to have the resources to maintain health care free at the point of use.

The reason it is possible to sustain the health and education levels is simple: political will, which has been the basis of 50 years of working to improve social welfare. Although it is difficult to believe, in our island the economic sphere is actually quite distinct from social achievements in health, sport and education. All this is due to a determined government and decades of political will, which is bearing fruit.

Emulating Cuba

I wouldn't agree with my friend on all of his views, but they give pause for thought. What happens to the Cuban economy in the short term, let ... [alone] the long term, is something we watch with interest. But the kind of political will that sees health and education as a priority whatever the economic circumstances, and as an investment in economic growth rather than a cost to society, is one that other countries should emulate.

> *"Hundreds of thousands of Cubans live in substandard free housing. They line up to receive government rations of chicken, rice, and even sugar."*

Cubans Accept, Adapt to Their Iron-Hard Lives

Frank Barnako

Frank Barnako is a columnist for MarketWatch and the co-founder of a number of Internet ventures. In the following viewpoint, he argues that Cuba's people are trapped with a low and, in many ways, decaying standard of living. He points to aging cars and the lack of efficient postal service or Internet access. Barnako says that many Cubans have grown up under the current government and know no other kind of life. He says that Cubans generally accept and adapt to the country's poverty, but few expect it to change.

As you read, consider the following questions:

1. Why are there almost no new cars in Cuba, according to Barnako?

2. What did government ration books stop covering in January 2012, and what effect did this have on prices, according to Barnako?

3. Of what are Cubans fiercely proud, according to Barnako?

Havana, Cuba—It's as if this city has been preserved in amber.

Little appears to have changed in Cuba's capital since Fidel Castro took power in January 1959. The city's gorgeous but decaying Spanish-influenced colonial architecture casts shade on the streets of Old Havana.

General Motors dinosaurs of the '40s and '50s roam the plazas in search of visitors to taxi to the Hotel Nacional de Cuba, from which the Mafia ran the city in the old days.

Whether parked in front of high-end hotels or up on blocks on the side streets of Old Havana, the hundreds of mid-century Chevys, Buicks and Plymouths can't help but jolt American visitors of a certain age into memory land.

It's not that the climate of Cuba is so mild that the cars don't rust out, because they do. But, since Fidel's victory, Cubans have been forbidden to buy new cars. So the streets are full of pre-'60s iron—some of them looking showroom-new, some of them flaking and rattling. But all of them valuable because they are already here.

There has been change.

Cubans' standard of living has deteriorated, thanks to the Communist government and the U.S. trade embargo, and the disappearance of the Soviet Union's economic aid. Hundreds of thousands of Cubans live in substandard free housing. They line up to receive government rations of chicken, rice and even sugar.

The postal service is slow, expensive and unreliable. Home telephones are all but nonexistent. Internet access is severely restricted and mostly reserved for the government and the tourist hotels. On the street, even a casual conversation can prompt a Cuban's criticism of Fidel and the government. This is Cuba today.

The monthly rations are distributed in small, neighborhood shops. People line up 10 or 15 deep for their allocations of beans, eggs, a chicken, coffee and rice. Well-worn blackboards propped in the corners of the store guide families' "shopping" and menu planning. Even toilet paper appears to be in short supply, evidenced by the well-dressed woman walking down a street tightly holding on to a roll.

In January, government ration books stopped covering "personal cleanliness products," the Associated Press reported. The price of a bar of soap rose from 8 cents U.S. to 56 cents; toothpaste went from 20 cents to 88 cents, according to media reports. These are not small increases in a country where government employees are paid $8 to $20 a month.

Accept and Adapt

In typical fashion, however, Cubans accept and adapt. Elias Conde, a father of two who works in a cafeteria, told the Associated Press, "We're used to them taking things away. Tomorrow it'll be something else."

You might ask how Cubans can live with this. The easy answer is, they have no choice. They are resigned. With a median age of 38 years according to the CIA, a great deal of the country has known things only the way they are. It's always been this way.

Which brings us to Almando and Carlio, father and son, working on their car. Actually, it's Carlio's car. He's a taxi driver, but because the 1950 Chevy is out of order, he's out of business.

His father, Almando, however, is a mechanic. A year younger than La Revolución, he has only known Castro's government. In fact, he works for it, managing the automotive-repair shop where he is helping his son fix the taxi.

He uses gasoline to wash and clean an engine block. "Made in Russia," he says with a smile. It will take him about a week to get the car back on the road, he said. Much of the time reviving the vehicle will be spent hand-making parts. There are no AutoZone stores. Almando's best tools are imagination, ingenuity and inventiveness.

Carlio drives his cab six days a week, 7 A.M. to 10 P.M. His English is very good. He graduated from college and trained to be a lawyer. But opportunity, like food and freedom in Cuba, is in short supply. So he drives the cab. After expenses, he lives "a little better" than his government-employee father. He indicates how much better by a small gap between his thumb and forefinger.

A Warm Welcome

The Cuban people are welcoming. "Where you from?" is their first question. "How you like Cuba?" is the second. They realize life is harder for them than for the 1.2 million Cuban-Americans as close as 90 miles away. They are also fiercely proud of Cuba's culture of art, dance, architecture, athletics (boxing and baseball) and music.

There is debate and curiosity about what will happen after Fidel Castro—called El Gato' by Blanco, a gymnasium attendant—dies. "Things should change: There is a lack of opportunity," he told a reporter on the street while sipping coffee from a plastic cup.

"But I don't think they will."

> "Despite state achievements like low in-
> fant mortality and high literacy rates,
> this group . . . wants something more,
> and they believe they can get it some-
> where else."

Cubans Do Not Accept Their Low Standard of Living

Amelia Rosenberg Weinreb

Amelia Rosenberg Weinreb is a lecturer in the Department of Anthropology at the University of Texas at Austin. In the follow-ing viewpoint, she argues that many middle-class Cubans are frustrated with the country's low standard of living and poor economy. She says that such people often engage in black market activities and go around the law to make ends meet for their families. She says that many are angry at the government and are very aware of the consumer goods and opportunities that they cannot access. She says that many of them are also aware of, and actively consider, emigrating illegally.

As you read, consider the following questions:

1. Who does Weinreb identify as her "protagonists"?

2. Why does Weinreb say that most Cuban families she studied were small?

3. Why does Weinreb say that the middle-class citizen-consumers she discusses have been overlooked by anthropologists and researchers?

Summer morning. Residential neighborhood. Havana, Cuba.

Garments dry quickly in the morning sun, and are best brought indoors by midday to avoid the daily frenzy of unpegging at the first roll of afternoon thunder. This is when women call out, announcing the arrival of rain and, as a neighborly gesture, yank down all nearby laundry from the communal clothesline. Cubans, who excel at guarding their private lives from one another, and who take care not to air their dirty laundry in public, still engage in a lot of friendly handling of other people's clean laundry. They also spend a lot of time sharing lines—not only clotheslines, but also phone lines, ration lines, pharmacy lines, shopping lines, faltering factory production lines, and one-party lines.

I am privy to certain conversations because I share a clothesline with Tatiana and Petra, who have been living two doors down from each other on the same passageway for five years, and who do trust each other—as far as Cuban neighbors ever do. Squinting and starting to sweat, I listen to them chat as clothes go up for the day, about the influence of their astrological signs on their personalities, the going rate for home manicures and pedicures, the declining quality of public school lunches, and—quite aggravating to Tatiana—the fact that the price of Nestlé Nesquik flavored milk has just gone up, yet again. Her complaint does not resonate with nostalgic images of Cubans receiving Communist no-brand rations in tin cups. In fact, Tatiana regards chocolate-flavored Nesquik (a Mexican import) as a household staple for her school-aged daughter, and the price hike is going to place an added strain on the family purse. "But," she adds, lowering her voice, a Cuban citizen's ritual indexing the moment when a political problem enters the arena, "I can't say anything," she hisses in frustration, "Who would I complain to?" She throws up her hands, shrugs, and then slaps her cutoff jeans.

Unsatisfied Citizen-Consumers

The protagonists of this [viewpoint] are ordinary Cuban families quietly in search of a life with basic luxuries. Their search appears unremarkable, since neither their poverty nor their desires are extreme. They do not live terribly, they are not starving, but they work hard, and they want to live better. They long for affordable, quality goods and services that they believe are available elsewhere, they are frustrated with nationalized systems offering less than ever before, and they harbor resentment over their hard and unrewarded work. However, they explicitly avoid political activism as a tool to raise their standard of living. They prefer ritualized civic participation (or civic withdrawal), engagement in the informal economy, and undocumented migration as practical, clandestine strategies that circumvent or extend beyond the reach of state control.

Despite state achievements like low infant mortality and high literacy rates, this group, whom I call "unsatisfied citizen-consumers," wants something more, and they believe they can get it somewhere else. They often have remarkable firsthand details about specific types of goods and services they would like to access, for example Johnson's Baby Shampoo No More Tears formula, queen-sized pantyhose, home mortgage deals, fast Internet connections, and short lines at well-stocked medical centers.

The imported products increasingly available on shelves in shops in Havana remain prohibitively expensive for most Cubans, but as before, they continue to obtain awareness of consumer goods through hand-delivered gifts, visits and phone calls from family abroad, commercials broadcast on illegal satellite TV, conversations with tourists, and even videotaped footage of loved ones enjoying life in other countries. Such consumer details are politically symbolic, igniting vivid imaginings of life elsewhere and fueling subdued anger against the state. Ordinary citizens unavoidably experience stress and secrecy in trying to make ends meet in Cuba's authoritarian bureaucratic structure, obtain basic luxuries under the table, and discreetly plan their escape. These desires and pressures lie at the core of their lived experience.

I argue that unsatisfied citizen-consumers' political silence, underground economic activity, and secret identity as prospective migrants mark the boundaries of a significant "shadow public." This term plays on the common, parallel phrase "shadow economy," [referring to a black market, operating outside the legal system] as it also indicates informality and underground activity. Unlike what is generally considered "the public," however, a shadow public is a large group with common interests and concerns, but one that is non-united and seeks invisibility as its members look to improve their lot. . . .

And Cuba's circumstances are changing. Everything I describe is unfolding in Cuba's era of late socialism: a confluence of socialist bureaucracy with a social, economic, and cultural turn towards capitalist modes of consumption and production. . . . Late socialism serves as the backdrop for both a local sense of transformation and an unending stagnation that leads to citizen-consumer dissatisfaction and, consequently, to the development of a shadow public in Cuba.

Neighborhood Context

There is nothing shadowy about the neighborhoods of the shadow public. Informants directed me to and gave me tours of residential areas they recommended as economical, safe, decent, and "authentic." There was a simple code. By "economical, safe, and decent," informants were referring to communities that broke the stereotypical portrait of regional poverty: dirt, crime, delinquency, and marginality. Rather, they reflected a sort of "Middle America," Cuban style. These neighborhoods were further marketed to me, a prospective renter with a young family in tow, as populated by *buena gente* (families of respectable, kind, quality people, and in this context implicitly "white"), who would be good neighbors to us and would welcome us because we were, ostensibly, like them. "Es un barrio muy Cubano" (It's a very Cuban neighborhood), they would say, describing areas relatively unfrequented by tourists.

Consequently, . . . [much of the research for this project took] place in a leafy, middle-income, primarily residential neighborhood I will call "Los Árboles," which contains modest and mostly shabby apartment buildings and houses, and is located just outside the capital city center. Like most Havana neighborhoods, this one has its own small shopping strip with "dollar" stores (where goods must be purchased in U.S. dollars), a small outdoor farmers' market, a *consultorio* (medical practice) with a family doctor, pharmacies, schools, *bodegas* (ration distribution centers), and municipal headquarters. It is tied to Havana's city center, which is within easy traveling distance, for taking care of bureaucratic transactions, obtaining consumer supplies, and for some, going to work each morning. Yet Los Árboles and its residents lie outside both the popular and scholarly imagination of Cuban life. The area is described dismissively in travel guides in such terms as "it doesn't offer much to persuade you to linger" and "you wouldn't miss anything if you didn't drive through." Nor does the neighborhood represent an obvious center of "socialist exotica" or the "fallen grandeur" of *solares*, the Spanish colonial structures battered by the tropical elements where tourists feel they have stumbled upon the "real" Cuba.

If urban and suburban communities like Los Árboles are unremarkable, they are also pleasant in their unremarkability. Los Árboles is clean and tree-lined, and its longer-term residents are friendly and do not cause one another trouble. No matter the relative size or exterior condition of the dwellings (sometimes neighboring houses are in quite different states of repair), and despite socialist or egalitarian principles, the tidy interiors of these relatively modern, nuclear family homes usually feature a TV/VCR, a stereo, a pantry stocked with food and household cleaning products from the supermarket, and a bathroom cupboard containing a stash of pharmaceuticals and beauty aids. On their walls are framed photos of family members, mass-produced artwork, and sometimes a cross, expressing a moderate connection to Catholicism. They also typically have a modest collection of clothing and children's toys and other trappings of the modern "bourgeois" household—*electrodo-mésticos* such as blenders, air conditioners and washing machines—even if such trappings have unusual origins or histories of acquisition, which they almost always do.

This veneer of comfortable living belied the fact that most of my informants were cyclically cash poor and expended what they considered unreasonable amounts of time and energy perfecting the art of finding more, stretching their resources, and milking national systems. During hard times, employment provided them with a sense of legitimacy as rightful citizens and frustration as consumers with what they felt were punitively tight limitations, fueling negative feelings about how they lived, where they lived, and who was to blame for their situation.

Providing for the Family

Determining who is at fault becomes a particularly heated issue when parents are unable to provide what they want for their children. This inability shapes parents' worldviews painfully and profoundly, making families with children more likely to fit the characterization of unsatisfied citizen-consumers. In Cuba, as in most countries, families are the primary focus of national laws protecting and providing for citizens; the Código de Familia (Family Code) specifically outlines, among other things, the rights and responsibilities of families regarding their own children, and informs families of what the state is obligated to provide in turn. Guarantees of health care and education outlined in national constitutions are particularly valued by families, but unsatisfied citizen-consumers generally regard these provisions as just one crucial means of stretching their income. These benefits are not what citizens live on, they are not what they used to be, and they are not sufficient reason to show excessive deference to the state; on the other hand, nor are they considered an appropriate reason to organize collectively against the state.

Providing for their children means that families are forced to live in the present moment, taking care of immediate emotional and material needs, while also thinking about their children's futures. These citizen-consumers intentionally keep their families small. Regardless of the number of children they would ideally like, unsatisfied citizen-consumers commonly prevent further hardship by adhering strictly to birth-control regimens (and occasionally abortions funded by state clinics), unconfident that they could provide materially for more than one or two carefully spaced children in any dignified way, given their insecure personal financial circumstances and national economic realities. Sharing many consumption practices, they commiserate over line items on their budget and a special set of economic burdens and stressful financial cycles as they scrape together funds for birthdays, holidays, and school-related events.

When they have insufficient funds to provide for their children, they become more inventive, often engaging in illegal activities, which heighten their awareness of the state as an oppositional watchdog. Thus, families become embroiled in a cycle of vertical responsibility: their responsibilities to their children, and those the state has toward them.

Staying Afloat

Despite these frustrations, the unsatisfied citizen-consumers were quick to admit that others had it worse than they did. Informants would distinguish themselves from the truly poverty-stricken, saying things like, "¡Pero imagínete si yo fuera pobre!" (But imagine if I were poor!), or more often, "Si yo no tuviera dólares . . ." (if I didn't have dollars), expressing relief not to be in that category, which would provoke even more hardship. Indeed, because of a combination of legal and clandestine employment, state subsidies, and remittances and other gifts from abroad, none of the unsatisfied citizen-consumer families I discuss experienced extreme or prolonged difficulty subsisting, and they worked diligently to keep it that way.

In fact, at least one of the adults in each of the households I describe held gainful employment, even if only in a constitutionally guaranteed state position. More typically, the head of household (usually but not always the husband) held some sort of full-time work, and at least one family member also contributed to family income *por la izquierda* (literally "on the left"), meaning through self-employment in the form of small off-the-books, untaxed jobs, such as baking and selling cakes from home; peddling clothing, farm-fresh food, or bootleg CDs door-to-door; or running a hair salon out of a back room of their home. Other times, the family were *bisneros* (slang for black marketeers), with much more extensive engagement in a black-market business such as running a lucrative home-based restaurant with lobster on the menu, or selling bottles of rum pilfered from a state factory line.

Even if the combination of activities and income sources helped them and their families stay afloat, many felt that they were wasting their training and education; many had earned state-subsidized university degrees, and occasionally even higher degrees. Instead of applying their skills in a fruitful, legal job market, these unsatisfied citizen-consumers lived with the daily stress of maintaining an underground enterprise, facing the contradiction of wanting to provide a decent lifestyle for themselves and their families and of wanting to earn their own keep, but having no choice but to do so extralegally. Their aspirations were chronically frustrated, and they rendered themselves without the possibility of building a satisfying life, and therefore *sin futuro* (without a future), at least in Cuba.

Ordinary Outlaws

While unsatisfied citizen-consumers sometimes do not know specifically who the other members are—their constituency is very large and its boundaries very unclear—individual members of the group still share a general sense that they are normal and that they represent a majority. They refer to themselves and their condition as those of *la gente de la calle* (the "man on the street," or "everyday people"). Furthermore, most unsatisfied citizen-consumers, despite their involvement in illegal activities, are otherwise "clean-living"—they have immaculate homes; ironed clothing; well-scrubbed children; strong moral orientation in the areas of generosity, manners, propriety, thrift, industriousness, and conscientiousness; a desire for self-reliance; intense family loyalty; and sometimes (but not always) religious belief and observance.

Although Cuban unsatisfied citizen-consumers did not fit the typical portrait of outlaws, they were aware that they had excluded honesty and rule-following from their moral universe in the interest of coping materially. They were also troubled by certain elements of these choices. They described experiencing a dissonance between their personal values and the strategies they employed in order to earn a living informally or illegally—talking about how they had become largely numb to corruption and living outside the law, and how the constraint and apprehensions of their lives were fatiguing. They also described how their personal identities, against their will, had become wrapped up in thrift and stress related to maintaining financial security by illegal means, at the expense of all other individual interests.

I introduce, in short, an analytic category of people who are a key presence in Cuba but who remain a missing piece of the puzzle for understanding its transition into late socialism. This may be in part because anthropologists have tended to overlook "un-alluring," or majority, groups "hidden in plain sight" [in the words of Micaela Di Leonardo] even when their views and experiences are remarkably important for theorizing a concept. Middle-class non-elites do not "deserve" or warrant research like the poor do, and therefore there is little moral imperative to investigate their interests, as is made evident by their near invisibility in publications and academic discourse, particularly in contrast with the abundant anthropological literature and discourse on poverty in Latin America. . . .

While I use *citizen-consumer* . . . to emphasize the connection between citizen and consumer, there are times when it is clearer to separate the roles. Examples are when I describe how the dissatisfactions of my informants are specifically political, in terms of citizen dissatisfaction with national policy; shortcomings of the late-socialist welfare state; and problems such as lack of personal liberties, perceptions of heavy taxation, and absence of venues for complaint. On the other hand, these "citizen problems" often blend with consumer dissatisfactions, such as unpredictable household income expenditures and access to basic foodstuffs and articles of daily use, shortages, inconveniences, and low quality of local services, which often figure more prominently than citizen issues in everyday discourse. Together, the blended citizen and consumer complaints reflect on the welfare state's inability to provide, and lead to a collective disenchantment with home, lack of motivation to abide by the law, disengagement with the state, and ultimately migration.

Periodical and Internet Sources Bibliography

The following articles have been selected to supplement the diverse views presented in this chapter.

BBC News	"Human Rights in Cuba Deteriorate, Warns Amnesty," March 22, 2012. http://news.bbc.co.uk.
Boston.com	"Cuba Looks Back—and Forward," April 20, 2011.
Economist	"The Castros, Cuba and America: On the Road Towards Capitalism," March 24, 2012.
Ivet González	"Cuban Activists Defend Sexual Rights as Human Rights," Inter Press Service, May 17, 2012. www.ipsnews.net.
Juan Carlos Hidalgo	"Cuba Needs a Swift Transition Towards Capitalism," *Cato at Liberty*, September 14, 2010. www.cato-at-liberty.org.
Carol Hills	"Cuban Blogger Gets Government's Attention," *PRI's The World*, May 5, 2011. www.theworld.org.
Jorge Martin	"Where Is Cuba Going? Towards Capitalism or Socialism?," *In Defence of Marxism*, September 17, 2010. www.marxist.com.
Amanda Rivkin	"The Second Age of Castro," *Foreign Policy*, April 9, 2010.
Larry Rohter	"In Cuba, the Voice of a Blog Generation," *New York Times*, July 5, 2011.
Stephen Wilkinson	"Cuba: From Communist to Co-Operative?," *Guardian*, September 10, 2010.

OPPOSING
VIEWPOINTS®
SERIES

CHAPTER 2

What Is Cuba's Relationship with the World?

Chapter Preface

One of Cuba's most reported and controversial international alliances has been with Iran. The Iranian regime has been singled out for international sanctions because of its alleged pursuit of nuclear weapons technology as well as its repressive domestic policies. Cuba, too, has been the target of sanctions from the United States because of its authoritarian policies. The friendship between Cuba and Iran has thus been cause for concern in the United States.

Jeff Franks, writing in a January 12, 2012, article for Reuters, reported that Cuban president Raúl Castro, former leader Fidel Castro, and Iranian president Mahmoud Ahmadinejad met in early 2012 to discuss common policy goals and confirm their alliance. Franks reported that the two countries agreed on the peaceful use of nuclear energy and spoke out against economic sanctions, such as those that have been used against both nations. According to Franks, Ahmadinejad said of relations between Iran and Cuba, "Our positions, versions, interpretations are alike, very close. We have been good friends, we are and will be, and we will be together forever."

US representative Ileana Ros-Lehtinen (R-FL), chairman of the House Foreign Affairs Committee, argued in a January 11, 2012, statement quoted on the committee's website that the Iran/Cuba relationship was dangerous to the United States. "Both Iran and Cuba have clear intentions of harming the U.S., and both support extremist groups dedicated to bringing destruction to our nation or destabilizing our allies," Ros-Lehtinen argued. She said that Iranian loans would prop up the Cuban economy, and she also warned that the two countries were working together on biotechnology projects that could be used to create weapons. She said that they were also sharing intelligence "that could harm the United States and our allies."

On the other hand, Walid Zafar argued in a February 7, 2012, article on the *Political Correction* blog that alarmist views of the Iran-Cuba alliance are an overreaction. He pointed out that the Iran-Cuba relationship is not new and that Cuba trades with most of the world; the US embargo is not an international policy. He added that Cuba does not in fact support international terrorism, so concerns about Iran and Cuba jointly funding or promoting terrorism are overblown and unrealistic.

The Cuba-Iran relationship is an important one, but of course Cuba has close links with many other nations as well. Authors of the viewpoints in the following chapter look at some of those other vital relationships, including Cuba's ties to Venezuela, Canada, and Russia.

> *"Moscow has been signaling that it wants to restore a long relationship with Havana that included not only economic ties but also military and intelligence cooperation."*

Moscow-Havana Ties Worry US

Paul Richter

Paul Richter is a staff writer for the Los Angeles Times. *In the following viewpoint, he reports that Russia and Cuba had close military and intelligence ties during the Cold War. After the collapse of the Soviet Union in the early 1990s, these links ended, but they are being renewed as Russia begins to reassert its influence around the world, Richter says. He reports that some officials are concerned that Russian military and intelligence outposts in Cuba could signal a return to Cold War tensions and might compromise US security.*

As you read, consider the following questions:

1. Richter reports that Russia is unlikely to place nuclear weapons on Cuba. What does he report it will do instead?

2. Why does Richter say Russia is negotiating with Syria?

3. How large was, and how many Russians worked at, the intelligence complex at Lourdes, Cuba, according to Richter?

Some officials see Russian statements as bluster, but others are concerned about a new Cuban alliance.

Washington—Amid rising tensions over Georgia, U.S. officials are increasingly concerned that Russia is moving to rebuild one of the most dangerous features of the old Soviet Union's security structure—its alliance with Cuba.

Moscow has been signaling that it wants to restore a long relationship with Havana that included not only economic ties but also military and intelligence cooperation. The relationship brought the world to the brink of nuclear war during the Cuban missile crisis of 1962, when Russia secretly installed nuclear missiles on the island.

U.S. officials believe that Russian statements are partly bluster, intended to dissuade the United States and its allies from moving the NATO alliance and military equipment, including missile defense sites, closer to the Russian border. And some experts question how interested Cuba is in rebuilding close ties with Russia.

But at a time when Russia has intervened forcefully in Georgia and is extending the global reach of its rebuilt military, some senior officials fear it may not be only bluster.

Russia "has strategic ties to Cuba again, or at least, that's where they're going," a senior U.S. official said recently, speaking, like others, on condition of anonymity because of the sensitive implications of the assessments.

The officials said they doubted the Russians would risk stationing nuclear bombers on Cuba. But some believe that Moscow might seek to restore its once-energetic intelligence cooperation with Havana, and to resume limited military co-operation, possibly including refueling stops for aircraft and warships.

In the current environment, such contacts would make U.S. officials uneasy, serving as a reminder of a military relationship between Havana and Moscow that stretched from the Cuban revolution in 1959 until a weakened, post-Soviet Russia finally closed a massive electronic intelligence complex in Lourdes near Havana in 2001.

One senior military officer said a return of Russian ships or planes could force additional U.S. deployments in the region. But the Bush administration and Pentagon declined to comment publicly on the implications.

"It is very Cold War retro," said a government official. "The topic could be reminiscent of the Cuban missile crisis, and that is a chapter that people don't want to revisit."

The Russian Defense Ministry dismissed a report in the newspaper *Izvestia* in July that quoted an unidentified Russian official as saying the government intended to begin basing Tupolev Tu-160 Blackjack and Tupolev Tu-95 Bear nuclear bombers in Cuba.

However, the report was taken seriously enough in Washington that Gen. Norton A. Schwartz, the new air force chief of staff, said during his Senate confirmation hearing at the time that sending the bombers would cross a "red line in the sand."

Last month, Secretary of State Condoleezza Rice complained about Russia's increasing reliance on its military to remind the world of its power. She criticized Russia's military advance into Georgia, a former Soviet republic, and its increasingly frequent patrols by long-range nuclear bombers in U.S.- and NATO-patrolled ocean lanes near northern Europe, Alaska and elsewhere.

As it rebuilds forces that withered during the impoverished 1990s, Russia also has been looking for new air and naval bases far from home. It is negotiating with Syria to resume use of naval bases in Tartus and Latakia, Russian officials have said. There has also been talk in Moscow of approaching Vietnam about using Cam Ranh Bay.

Russian Prime Minister Vladimir Putin in late July sent one of his closest aides, Deputy Prime Minister Igor Sechin, and a large delegation to meet with Cuban President Raúl Castro. The meeting was primarily about economic cooperation, including possible oil exploration off Cuba. But Russian officials made it clear that they were exploring resumption of other aspects of the relationship as well.

Nikolai Patrushev, who is secretary of the Russian Security Council and former director of the FSB, the domestic successor agency to the KGB, met with the Cuban defense and interior ministers on the trip. Afterward, the council issued a statement saying that the two countries planned "consistent work to restore traditional relations in all areas of cooperation."

Afterward, Putin said, "We need to reestablish positions in Cuba and in other countries."

Some Russian analysts remain skeptical of the Kremlin's intentions, seeing the whispers of renewed military activity in Cuba as a tactic meant to rattle the United States.

Russian officials "understand that the restoration of even an intelligence-gathering base in Lourdes would be a declaration of a new Cold War on the part of Russia," said Alexander Golts, defense analyst with the online publication *Yezhednevny Zhurnal*. "The Kremlin will never do it, because they cannot afford it."

Despite talk of a return to the Cold War, Golts noted, Russia spends 2.7% of its gross domestic product on defense—unlike the Soviet Union, which at the height of the Cold War spent 40%.

The Russian Military and Georgia

Russia is still one of the two great nuclear powers in the world, possessing nearly half of the world's nuclear weapons. However, the modernization of Russian military forces has proceeded slowly; its core missile force is aging and its conventional military force is largely outmoded. [President Vladimir] Putin succeeded in reviving somewhat of the Russian militarist tradition and increasing military spending. . . . From 2008, Russia began to acquire new military hardware such as nuclear submarines, strategic bombers, ballistic missiles, and tanks. Its efforts appear to be focused on building a strong internal security apparatus and the military capacity to win small wars, which reflect the country's most probable sources of danger: low-level internal conflicts and small-scale actions nearby. . . .

Russia largely avoided military action until the summer 2008 Georgia crisis [in which Georgia responded] to Russian flights over the separatist province of South Ossetia by threatening to shoot down its planes. By early August, Russia responded to Georgia's deployment of troops in South Ossetia's capital, Tskhinvali, by launching an air attack on Georgian troops near the city of Gori, and then sending tanks into Georgia and engaging in bombing raids near its capital, Tbilisi. . . . Many analysts see Russia's actions as a signaling effort to countries of the former Soviet Union of its interest in maintaining a sphere of influence in the region and countering the United States and NATO expansion.

Vinod K. Aggarwal and Kristi Govella, eds. "Introduction: The Fall of the Soviet Union and the Resurgence of Russia," Responding to a Resurgent Russia: Russian Policy and Responses from the European Union and the United States. *New York: Springer, 2012.*

Although several Bush administration officials who have been hawkish on Russia say they find the Cuba ties worrisome, other U.S. officials say the threat should not be overstated.

"The old days are gone, and people need to keep a sense of perspective," said one U.S. official. "That said, I wouldn't assume these [Cuban and Russian intelligence] services never talk to each other."

That official said Cuban intelligence activities posed a concern even without rekindled Russian ties.

"They were and are aggressive on their own," he said. "If anything, the years that have passed since the end of the Soviet Union have convinced the Cubans that, when it comes to intelligence, they themselves are the only people on whom they can rely."

Since becoming president, Raúl Castro has generally avoided provoking the United States, said Brian Latell, a former CIA analyst and Cuba specialist. Latell said he was skeptical that Castro would want to be caught in the middle of the rekindled U.S.-Russian rivalry.

"Why go out on a limb for Putin?" asked Latell, who has written a book, *After Fidel*, about Cuba's political transition. "I'm not sure I can discern why the Cubans would want to get themselves wrapped around these great power issues."

Latell added, though, that he was ready to believe that the Cubans would cooperate on intelligence and would resume limited military contacts, such as refueling of aircraft.

The 28-square-mile Russian electronic surveillance complex at Lourdes was Russia's largest such base overseas, and reportedly had as many as 1,500 Russian engineers, technicians and military personnel working there. Less than 100 miles from Key West, Fla., its position made it ideal for snooping on the U.S.

The Russian government ended its involvement there in 2001 because of its high cost as well as the strain it exerted on U.S.-Russian relations.

Mark Hackard, assistant director of the Nixon Center in Washington, said Russia's moves grew out of its sense that, although it has given ground on security again and again since the 1990s, it has received little in return from the United States and its allies. Yet, there are limits to how far the Russians will extend their military, he said.

"They're not seeking a new superpower standoff around the world," Hackard said. "They do want primacy in the former Soviet sphere."

> *"Russia has no nuclear weapons on Cuba, no weapons. The relationship between Russia and the United States is not a threat for us."*

Cuba's Ties with Russia Are Not a Danger to the United States

Evgenij Haperskij

Evgenij Haperskij is a research associate at the Council on Hemispheric Affairs. In the following viewpoint, he reviews the history of ties between Russia and Cuba. He explains that the Soviet Union and Communist Cuba maintained important economic and strategic ties until the collapse of the Soviet Union in the early 1990s. The withdrawal of Russian aid caused great hardship in Cuba; however, he says, today Russia and Cuba are moving closer together again. He concludes, however, that the Russian-Cuban alliance today poses no threat to the United States. Therefore, he says, the United States should end its economic embargo against Cuba.

As you read, consider the following questions:

1. According to Haperskij, what involvement did the United States have in Cuba before the Cuban revolution?

Evgenij Haperskij, "Cuba—Russia Now and Then," Council on Hemispheric Affairs, February 24, 2010. Copyright © 2010 by Council on Hemispheric Affairs. All rights reserved. Reproduced by permission.

2. What does Haperskij say the Soviet Union delivered to Cuba between 1959 and 1991?

3. What relationships does Haperskij say are more important to Russia and Cuba than their trade partnership?

Years after the collapse of the Soviet Union and the associated termination of cooperation and a strong alliance between Cuba and Russia, both states are now working overtime to revive the relationship which once brought the world to the brink of nuclear war when the Soviet Union covertly installed nuclear missiles on the Caribbean island. It is hardly surprising that Russia's attempts to revive its relationship with the former ally are being closely monitored by the U.S., seeing that Russia and Cuba have a shared legacy and due to Cuba's proximity to Washington. Presently, however, Russia is not attempting to develop a relationship based on ideological confrontation, but rather one based on economic pragmatism.

An Overview of Cuban Relations with Russia

Russian and Cuban ties originated many decades prior to Fidel Castro taking power. After Cuba's independence in 1902, the Russian Empire initiated diplomatic relations with Cuba. After the Russian Revolution in 1917, Cuba put the relationship on hold until 1943, when Russia was a major belligerent in the war against Nazi Germany. In 1952, [Fulgencio] Batista [the U.S.-backed authoritarian leader of Cuba in the 1940s and 1950s] again broke off its relationship with Moscow due to Russia's Communist affiliation. During this period and then after the Cuban revolution in 1959 and even after Fidel Castro's proud Communist cry, Cuba was not viewed by Moscow as being of particular importance to Russia. Soviet leadership realized that the island was squarely located in the U.S. sphere of influence and would be difficult to defend if challenged by the U.S.

Before the Cuban revolution in 1959, the United States had investments in Cuba totaling about one billion in U.S.-dollars, representing nearly twelve percent of all U.S. investments in Latin America. The Cuban economy at the time was completely dominated by its powerful neighbor, but everything changed after Fidel Castro came to power. He launched a land reform program and seized American assets, putting them under government control. In attempting to topple the Castro regime, the United States slashed its sugar quota for Cuba which heavily affected the Cuban economy. This measure did not result in a desired change in Cuban leadership, but effectively moved the island much closer politically to Moscow.

Castro Becomes a Communist

When Castro came to power in 1959, his revolutionary movement did not profess Communistic ideology, but only two years later, he announced that he was a Marxist Leninist and would remain so until his death. He also declared that the Integrated Revolutionary Organizations (IRO), the precursor of the Communist Party of Cuba, was formed by the merger of Fidel Castro's 26th of July Revolutionary Movement and the Socialist People's Party. Castro's political shift could be seen as one of economic necessity. After the revolution, the Cuban middle class, dissatisfied with the new leadership's political course, fled Cuba. This huge economic brain drain, coupled with the closure of the U.S. market to Cuban sugar, led to a precarious fiscal situation on the island.

The Soviet Union took advantage of the favorable situation for it to meddle and decided to come to Cuba's assistance on February 13, 1960. It did this in order to gain influence in the Western Hemisphere, marking the inauguration of the modern Cuban-Soviet relationship. Representatives from both leftist governments signed a trade agreement which became the basis for further economic cooperation. In this agreement, the Soviet Union committed to purchase 425,000 tons of sugar in 1960, and from 1961 to 1964 one million tons of sugar annually. Furthermore, [Soviet leader] Nikita Khrushchev granted Havana a 100 million U.S.-dollar credit at a very low interest (2.5%) and promised to sell oil to Cuba below world market prices. This enabled Cuba to once again rely on its sugar industry to buoy the Cuban economy because of Russia's guarantee of a stable market and further economic aid. As a result, Cuba became nearly totally dependent on the Soviet Union. In order for Cuba to receive financial subventions from Moscow, the Soviet Union demanded that Cuba make certain economic reforms. Just as Cuba reformed its economy to follow the Soviet Union's specifications, Cuba's political order was reformed as well. On the surface, Castro's regime became Marxist Leninist; in fact, he and his speeches framed the ideological guideline and not the working class or the party. However, through his formal commitment to communism, Castro won the abiding support and affection of the Soviet Union, even though its leaders barely comprehended him, thereby ensuring financial security for his island. Furthermore, the Soviet Union gained an ally in its Cold War against the United States located close to its borders. This alliance led to the most serious confrontation during the Cold War when Soviet and Cuban governments placed nuclear missiles on Cuban soil in 1962.

In the 1980s, Cuban dependence on the Soviet Union increased due to falling global oil prices between 1983 and 1985. Cuba, which once could sell a part of the cheap oil that it bought from Russia on the world market, was now finding it difficult to profit from the sale of its surplus oil. Thereafter, Cuba focused almost completely on trade with the Soviet Union and the other socialist countries by the late 1980s. Between 1959 and 1991, the Soviet Union delivered 170 million tons of oil, 13 million tons of grain, and 300,000 trucks, cars and tractors to Cuba. While Cuba's dependence on the Soviet

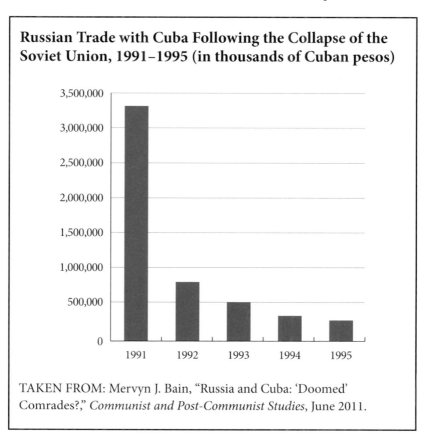

Russian Trade with Cuba Following the Collapse of the Soviet Union, 1991–1995 (in thousands of Cuban pesos)

TAKEN FROM: Mervyn J. Bain, "Russia and Cuba: 'Doomed' Comrades?," *Communist and Post-Communist Studies*, June 2011.

Union was growing, the latter began to gradually disassociate itself from the island. In an interview with a Cuban newspaper, [Fidel's brother, Cuban general, and later Cuban president] Raúl Castro revealed that the Soviet Union told Fidel during his visit to Moscow in 1983 that it would not defend Cuba if the U.S. was to attack the island. Both countries decided to keep this strategic shift secret. However, eight years later it was the Soviet Union which imploded and triggered the fall of Communist governments around the world.

Cuba's Survival After the Collapse of the Soviet Union

After the collapse of the Soviet Union, Russia immediately began to throw the switches on its traditional economic relations with Cuba. Russian officials began to distance themselves from Castro and began to support the anti-Castro emigration from Cuba. According to the Russian parliament (DUMA), the trade between Russia and Cuba decreased from nine billion in 1990 to 710 million U.S.-dollars three years later. From 1989 to 1991, Russian exports to Cuba fell by 70%. The oil exports fell twice between 1989 and 1992, resulting in the collapse of Cuba's foreign trade. During the course of its economic crisis, the social problems in Cuba were exacerbated. Power cuts, a lack of medicine, and the prevalence of a booming black market were symptoms of the economic crisis which peaked in 1993. However, through internal market reforms, Castro was able to keep his regime barely alive during what was known as the "Special Period," which was characterized by great deprivation and suffering.

Although Russia had reduced its cooperation with Cuba to a bare minimum, it never entirely ended the relationship and soon the de-acceleration was followed by first tentative efforts of a weak rapprochement. In November 1992, both countries signed agreements on trade and economic cooperation. In December 1993, an agreement on cultural and scientific cooperation was also initiated. In May 1996, the declaration on the principles of relationships between the Russian Federation and the Republic of Cuba outlined the desire to look for ways to resolve present economic frictions. Furthermore, critics increasingly began to voice their concerns over Russia's restrictive stance towards its former ally.

On October 14, 1994, members of the DUMA criticized the Russian de facto embargo against Cuba and appealed to the Russian leadership to revive the economic relationship with Havana. Simultaneously, it also called upon the United States to end the economic embargo against Cuba which had led to a social and economic catastrophe on the island. However, Washington did not even consider resolving its boycott against Cuba. Instead, after the collapse of Cuba's powerful sponsor, the United States decided to go for the kill by tightening the embargo in order to try to topple the Castro regime. In 1996, the [Bill] Clinton administration passed the Cuban Liberty [and Democratic Solidarity (Libertad)] Act, also known as the Helms-Burton Act [after Senator Jesse Helms and Representative Dan Burton]. Title III of this bitterly anti-Cuban initiative determined that the United States would prosecute countries "allegedly trafficking property formerly owned by U.S. citizens but expropriated by Cuba" after the 1959 revolution had been staged. Helms-Burton also contained a section referring to Russia, which after the collapse had retained its intelligence facilities on Cuban territory. This section refused any assistance to Russia in case it acted to [use] these facilities. Moscow backed Cuba in the UN [United Nations] vote against this act not wanting to close its intelligence facilities or end its economic relationship with Cuba. Instead of biding by the spirit of this act, Russia further sought to gradually foster the revival of its old relationship with its former ally.

Rapprochement of Former Allies

During the rule of [Russian president] Boris Yeltsin (1991–1999), the first bilateral agreements with Cuba were signed. However, Cuba was not seen as being particularly important for Russian foreign policy goals and trade continued to decrease between the two. Under the leadership of Vladimir Putin, Russia gradually changed course in its policies toward Cuba. In 2000, he visited and granted Castro a 50 million U.S.-dollar credit, a relatively meager financial aid package, but one that marked the resumption of an official dialogue between some of Cuba's and Russia's highest leaders. During his visit to Cuba, Putin emphasized that Russia had no ideological agenda in the region and instead wanted practical deals that would benefit Russian businesses, pointing to a pragmatic component of the relationship. One year later, following the introduction of this new stance, Putin closed the controversial Russian radar station in Cuba, complying with the U.S. demands that had angered many Cubans because of sovereignty issues. Nonetheless, under Putin, trade links between Cuba and Russia increased, from 125 million U.S.-dollars in 2005 to over 231 million in 2006 and then to 285 million, with the trade turnover peaking in 2007. These figures made Cuba the seventh largest Russian trading partner in Latin America (but represented only 0.05% of Russia's total foreign trade). More significant than the trade relationship between the former allies was the revival of their strategic partnership. In 2009, Russian deputy prime minister Igor Sechin signed four contracts securing exploration rights in Cuba's economic zone in Cuban territorial offshore waters, involving oil exploration in the Gulf of Mexico.

Nonetheless, for the United States, Russian involvement in Cuba is nothing to worry about. "Russia has no nuclear weapons on Cuba, no weapons. The relationship between Russia and the United States is not a threat for us," said Wayne Smith, senior fellow and director of the Cuba Project at the Center for International Policy. Even the Pentagon acknowledges that Cuba does not constitute a danger to U.S. public security. This raises the question why the United States is still clinging to the boycott against Cuba which has had no impact on Cuban policy thus far. Dr. Smith, who served as executive secretary of President [John F.] Kennedy's Task Force on Latin America and chief of mission at the U.S. Interests Section in Havana, criticizes the American stance toward Cuba: "It does not make any sense. But the United States is not prepared as of yet to deal rationally with Cuba. Cuba is not a threat and it has signaled that it wants to have a constructive dialogue, which is needed. Polls indicate that the majority of Americans are in favor of such dialogue," which has to leave the [U.S. president Barack] Obama administration a bit embarrassed by its false starts up to now.

> "*Cuban health workers, in addition to providing free health care for all their fellow citizens, have transformed themselves into a 'weapon of solidarity,' a revolutionary force that has been deployed in over 100 countries around the world.*"

Where Do Revolutionary Doctors Come From?

Steve Brouwer

Steve Brouwer is the author of numerous books, including Sharing the Pie: A Citizen's Guide to Wealth and Power. *In the following viewpoint, he says that Cuba has sent an army of doctors to Venezuela to bring medical care to the poor, especially in rural areas. In addition to providing care, Brouwer reports, the doctors train Venezuelan students so that in the future Venezuela's health care system can thrive without Cuban aid. Brouwer says the medical program has shown the moral superiority of the revolutionary governments of Cuba and Venezuela in the face of opposition from the capitalist United States.*

As you read, consider the following questions:

1. According to Brouwer, what is Medicina Integral Comunitaria?

2. What is Barrio Adentro, and what role do Cubans play in it, according to Brouwer?

3. What does Brouwer say the United States did when its economic blockade failed to make Latin American nations shun Cuba and Venezuela?

> The campesinos would have run, immediately and with unreserved enthusiasm, to help their brothers.
>
> —*Che Guevara,*
> *"On Revolutionary Medicine," 1960*

Even though he came to Cuba with a rifle slung over his shoulder and entered Havana in 1959 as one of the victorious commanders of the Cuban Revolution, he still continued to think of himself as a doctor. Five years earlier, the twenty-five-year-old Argentine had arrived in Guatemala and offered to put his newly earned medical degree at the service of a peaceful social transformation. Dr. Ernesto Guevara was hoping to find work in the public health services and contribute to the wide-ranging reforms being initiated by President Árbenz, but he never had much opportunity to work as a physician in Guatemala. Within months of his arrival, Árbenz's government was brought down by the military coup d'état devised by the United Fruit Company, some Guatemalan colonels, the U.S. State Department, and the CIA.

Che never lost sight of the value of his original aspiration—combining the humanitarian mission of medicine with the creation of a just society. When he addressed the Cuban militia on August 19, 1960, a year and a half after the triumph of the revolution, he chose to speak about "Revolutionary Medicine" and the possibility of educating a new kind of doctor.

A few months ago, here in Havana, it happened that a group of newly graduated doctors did not want to go into the country's rural areas and demanded remuneration before they would agree to go. . . .

But what would have happened if instead of these boys, whose families generally were able to pay for their years of study, others of less fortunate means had just finished their schooling and were beginning the exercise of their profession? What would have occurred if two or three hundred campesinos had emerged, let us say by magic, from the university halls?

What would have happened, simply, is that the campesinos would have run, immediately and with unreserved enthusiasm, to help their brothers.

Since then, Cuban medicine and health services have been developed in a number of unique and revolutionary ways, but only now, nearly fifty years later, has Che's dream come to full fruition. Today it is literally true that campesinos, along with the children of impoverished working-class and indigenous communities, are becoming doctors and running, "with unreserved enthusiasm, to help their brothers."

While this is happening on the mountainsides of Haiti, among the Garifuna people on the Caribbean coast of Honduras, in the villages of Africa and the highlands of Bolivia, it is occurring on the grandest scale in the rural towns and city barrios of Venezuela. When I was living in the mountains of western Venezuela in 2007 and 2008, I witnessed the emergence of revolutionary doctors every morning as I walked out the door of our little tin-roofed house. The scene would have delighted Che:

As the sun rises above the mountain behind the village of Monte Carmelo and the white mist begins to lift off the cloud forest, four young campesinos walk along the road in their wine-red polo shirts with their crisp white jackets folded up under their arms to protect them from the dust. At 7 a.m. they wave goodbye to the high school students who are waiting to begin their classes in three rooms at the women's cooperative and then hop aboard the "taxi," a tough, thirty-year-old Toyota pickup truck that often packs twenty or more people in the back. They travel down the winding mountain road, through the deep ravine at the bottom, and up the hill on the far side of the valley to the larger town of Sanare, where they are going to work all morning alongside Cuban doctors in neighborhood consulting offices and the modern Diagnostic Clinic.

Around 7:45, four more medical students from the village, already donning their white jackets, walk by our house, past the plaza and the little church, and gather in front of a small concrete block building called the *ambulatorio*. About the same time, they are joined by three more medical students who emerge from Carlos's bright blue jeep, "the Navigator," one of the other vehicles in the taxi cooperative that serves the village. These students from Sanare pull on their white jackets, hug their compañeros, and wait for Elsy, a health committee volunteer who is studying to be a nurse, to unlock the gate to the *ambulatorio*, the walk-in clinic that offers Barrio Adentro medical service.

As I stroll by, I see the prospective patients sitting on the benches of the small, covered patio in front of the entrance door. They are waiting for Dr. Tomasa, the family medical specialist. Two chirpy teenage girls sit next to Dr. Raul's dentistry room and grin with perfect-looking smiles. "What could be wrong with your teeth?" I ask.

"Nothing," responds one of them, "Dr. Raul is giving us another checkup." Another checkup? Their parents never had a single checkup when they were young—consequently, there are many people over forty or fifty who have very few teeth.

By 8 a.m., one of the medical students stands behind the simple wooden counter, performing receptionist duties. Another shuttles back and forth to the file shelves, organizing and updating medical information that is kept on every family in the community. A third chats informally with the waiting patients, entertaining their small children, and informally inquiring about their families' health. The other four students stand alongside Dr. Tomasa in the consulting office, watching her take family and individual histories and give examinations. They also fetch medicines, take temperatures, and weigh healthy children who are accompanying their mothers. Today, like every day, Dr. Tomasa says to her students, "*Por favor*, more questions. This is how we learn. You can never ask too many questions."

Monte Carmelo is a small village that stretches along a single paved road on a mountain ridge in the foothills of the Andes in the state of Lara. Before Hugo Chávez assumed the presidency of Venezuela in 1999, the road was unpaved and the high school did not exist. According to the 2007 census, its population consisted of 129 families and approximately 700 individuals, nearly all of them supporting themselves by working small parcels of land by hand, or with horses and oxen. That same year, nine residents of Monte Carmelo were medical students. Eight were studying Medicina Integral Comunitaria (popularly known as MIC), an intensive six-year course that in English is usually called comprehensive community medicine. A ninth village resident was studying medicine in Cuba. Two more young women from a neighboring hamlet were also in medical school. They were part of a group of sixty-seven students in this agricultural region who were becoming doctors of medicine.

The students are a diverse lot: Some are nineteen or twenty years old and have recently finished high school; others are closer to thirty and have young children; a few are even older. Some young mothers have recently completed their secondary education through Misión Ribas, one of the Bolivarian social missions that bring adults back to school on evenings and weekends. All of the students are enthusiastic about their role in fostering good health and introducing reliable medical care into the fabric of their community and the larger world. And many of them dream of emulating their Cuban teachers and one day serving as internationalist physicians themselves in remote and impoverished parts of the world.

This experiment in training new doctors in MIC would be worthy of international attention even if the program was limited to the 67 students in this remote coffee-growing region in the state of Lara. But in fact they represent only a tiny fraction of a gigantic effort to transform medical education and health care delivery throughout all of Venezuela. Nearly 25,000 students were enrolled in the first four years of MIC in 2007–2008, and by 2009 and 2010 they were joined by more students, swelling the ranks of students enrolled in all six years of MIC to approximately 30,000. This is almost as many as the total number of doctors who were practicing medicine in all capacities in Venezuela when Hugo Chávez was elected president in 1998.

One unique aspect of MIC is that the students in Monte Carmelo do not have to leave the *campo*, the countryside, nor do students in the poorest neighborhoods of Venezuelan cities have to desert their barrios in order to attend medical school. Medicina Integral Comunitaria is a "university without walls" that trains young doctors in their home environments. This is not a short-term course for health aides or "barefoot doctors," but a rigorous program designed to produce a new kind of physician. Every morning during their years of study, the MIC students help doctors working in Barrio Adentro attend to patients' illnesses and learn to comprehend the broad public health needs of their communities. And every afternoon, they meet with their MIC professors in a series of formal medical classes that constitute a rigorous curriculum and include all the medical sciences studied at traditional universities.

The MIC education program could not exist without Barrio Adentro, the nationwide health system that first began delivering primary care in 2003 thanks to an enormous commitment of expertise from Cuba. From 2004 to 2010, Barrio Adentro continually deployed between 10,000 and 14,000 Cuban doctors and 15,000 to 20,000 other Cuban medical personnel—dentists, nurses, physical therapists, optometrists, and technicians. Their services are available to all Venezuelans for free at almost 7,000 walk-in offices and over 500 larger diagnostic clinics, and they have been very effective in meeting the needs of 80 percent of the population that had been ill-served or not served at all by the old health care system.

Obviously, Cuba cannot afford to devote so many of its medical personnel to Venezuela indefinitely, nor does the Chávez government want to depend on foreign doctors forever. So when Barrio Adentro was being launched in 2003, Cuban and Venezuelan medical experts devised a new program of medical education that will enable Venezuela to keep its universal public health program functioning permanently. Starting in 2005, the Cuban doctors were asked to perform a rigorous double duty: not only did they continue treating patients in Barrio Adentro clinics, but many of them also began teaching as professor/tutors for the MIC program in comprehensive community medicine. The goal of MIC is to integrate the training of family practitioners into the fabric of communities in a holistic effort that meets the medical needs of all citizens, makes use of local resources, and promotes preventive health care and healthy living.

The Cuban mission in Venezuela is possible because over the past half century, Cuba has developed a vision of medical service that goes far beyond its own borders. Cuban health workers, in addition to providing free health care for all their fellow citizens, have transformed themselves into a "weapon of solidarity," a revolutionary force that has been deployed in over 100 countries around the world. Since 2000, however, the Cuban commitment has increased substantially because the Bolivarian Revolution in Venezuela has contributed its own enthusiasm, volunteers, and economic resources. Through various agreements of cooperation, Cuba and Venezuela have embarked upon a number of projects in other fields such as education, agriculture, energy, and industrial development, and then have extended these cooperative ventures to other nations, particularly within ALBA, the Bolivarian Alliance for the Peoples of Our America, which includes Bolivia, Nicaragua, and Ecuador as well as the small Caribbean island nations of Dominica, Antigua and Barbuda, Saint Vincent and the Grenadines.

Of all these ambitious undertakings, delivering medical services is by far the most prominent. In order to extend universal health care to the poor and working classes in a way that is compatible with the new, egalitarian vision of these societies, many more physicians are needed. With this in mind, Cuba is educating more doctors at home even as it trains tens of thousands in Venezuela. In 2008 there were 29,000 Cubans enrolled in medical school, plus nearly 24,000 foreign students (including more than one hundred students from the United States) studying at the Latin American School of Medicine in Havana or at the schools of the new program for the training of Latin American doctors that are located in four other provinces.

An Army in White Jackets

I first became aware of the magnitude of this medical revolution in 2004 on my first trip to Venezuela. When Dr. Yonel, a young Cuban dentist working in a barrio of Caracas, informed me there were more than 10,000 doctors working in Venezuela, I exclaimed, "*Un ejército de medicos!* An army of doctors!"

Dr. Yonel smiled and replied, "*Un ejército de paz.* An army of peace."

Clearly the collaboration of the rejuvenated Cuban revolution and the nascent Bolivarian Revolution was yielding impressive results. And a growing number of countries in the

Cuban Doctors in Guatemala

It is clear that, in Central America, Cuba continues to make an important contribution to the social development of its peoples. In the case of Guatemala, for instance, Cuban doctors have been working for nine years and are now in 17 of the nation's 22 provinces and in all there are almost 400 Cuban physicians at present in Guatemala. . . . Altogether, some 3,500 Cuban doctors have served there. In total, they have saved an estimated 270,000 lives, carried out 26 million consultations, and perforated 144,000 surgical operations—including 40,000 eye operations through Operation Miracle. In addition they have assisted at 70,712 births and have reduced by more than half both infant and maternal mortality rates in the locations where they are working. Current rates are 6.8 and 61.1 per thousand, respectively. What is particularly pleasing is to see the contribution in Guatemala of the 470 graduates of ELAM [Latin American School of Medicine], back home and working in their native land. A further 600 Guatemalan medical students are studying in Cuba and will return to their homeland after graduation.

John M. Kirk and H. Michael Erisman, Cuban Medical Internationalism: Origins, Evolution, and Goals. *New York: Palgrave Macmillian, 2009.*

Western Hemisphere, long under the yoke of wealthy conservative minorities or military authoritarians who were dependent on capital and political instruction from the North, were no longer willing to listen to the United States when it told them to shun Cuba and Venezuela. Since its long-standing economic blockade of Cuba was failing to deter these developments, the United States tried to launch a disruptive dissident movement in Cuba and assist a coup d'état in Venezuela. When these efforts failed, the U.S. government imposed more draconian economic and travel restrictions on Cuba in 2004 and funded various schemes to undermine both revolutionary governments. In 2006, the United States stooped to an especially low level when it attempted to directly sabotage Cuba's humanitarian medical missions by creating the Cuban Medical Professional Parole Program. This was a law specifically designed to lure Cuban doctors, nurses, and technicians away from their foreign assignments by offering them special immigration status and speedy entry into the United States.

These antagonistic efforts did not succeed in diminishing the international solidarity and prestige that Cuba and Venezuela were acquiring around the world, nor did it keep them from expanding their programs of humanitarian medical aid and international medical education. In 2007, a young Chilean, a member of the third class graduating from the Latin American School of Medicine in Havana, spoke at her commencement and told her classmates: "Today we are an army in white jackets that will bring good health and a little more dignity to our people."[1]

By 2010, Cuba and Venezuela further demonstrated their capabilities by being among the most prominent providers of both emergency and long-term aid to Haiti after its devastating earthquake. Brazil, the economic giant of Latin America, signaled its admiration by announcing that it would be delighted to join Cuba in a partnership to create a new public health system in Haiti. José Gomes, the Brazilian minister of health, explained why his country was choosing to work with the Cubans on such a significant and demanding project: "We have just signed an agreement—Cuba, Brazil, and Haiti— according to which all three countries make a commitment to

---

1. "Hoy somos un ejército de batas blancas que dará salud y un poco más de dignidad a nuestros pueblos." Dr. Katia Millaray, quoted in Rodolfo Romero Reyes, "Le nacen retornos a la salud publica cubana y latinomericana," http://www.almamater.cu, 2007.

unite our forces in order to reconstruct the health system in Haiti. . . . We will provide this, together with Cuba—a country with an extremely long internationalist experience, a great degree of technical ability, great determination, and an enormous amount of heart."[2]

For Cuba, Venezuela, and by extension their allies in the ALBA alliance, these triumphs throughout the first decade of the twenty-first century were more than diplomatic coups, they were moral victories. They demonstrated the power of social solidarity and humanistic concern for other people, values in stark contrast with the materialistic, self-centered, and aggressive behavior of the advanced capitalist societies.

2. Emily J. Kirk and John M. Kirk, "Cuban Medical Aid to Haiti," Counterpunch.com, April 1, 2010.

> "Raúl Castro is strongly interested in moving beyond an alliance built on personalities by creating sustainable, institutional arrangements, and this has helped to cement the Cuban-Venezuelan relationship."

Venezuelan Aid Has Helped Cuba's Economy

Marc Frank

Marc Frank is a correspondent for Reuters. In the following viewpoint, he reports that ties between Cuba and Venezuela have only grown closer since Raúl Castro replaced brother Fidel as president in 2006. Frank says that Venezuela has invested billions in Cuba. The Venezuelan investments have helped Cuba recover from the economic crisis that occurred after aid from the Soviet Union ceased in the early 1990s, according to Frank. The danger for Cuba now, Frank explains, is that it may become as dependent on Venezuela as it was on the Soviet Union, with disastrous results if relations between the two countries should worsen.

As you read, consider the following questions:

1. What is the nature of the oil-for-services deal between Venezuela and Cuba, according to Frank?

2. What is an example of a Venezuelan-Cuban joint venture that Frank describes?

3. What improvements in daily life does Frank say have resulted in Cuba from the partnership with Venezuela?

Speculation that Cuba's relations with Venezuela, its closest ally, might cool when Raúl Castro became president has disappeared as the countries have forged even deeper and broader ties.

An Alternative to Capitalism

Some experts thought Raúl Castro could not maintain the close relations his brother Fidel Castro had with his socialist protege, Venezuelan president Hugo Chávez, but the oil-rich South American country is investing billions of dollars in Cuba in increasingly complex ventures.

The two revolutionary allies aim to use the projects to reshape Latin America's political map by showing there is an alternative to capitalism and its main proponent, the United States.

They have an oil-for-services deal in which Venezuela ships 92,000 barrels a day to Cuba in exchange for the services of thousands of Cuban doctors and other technical assistance.

But they also reported more than 300 cooperation projects in 2007, and Venezuelan banks are financing 58 Cuban manufacturing programs and more than a dozen agricultural development schemes.

"Since the beginning, both Fidel Castro and Hugo Chávez have been determined to move the relationship between their countries beyond the oil-for-doctors swap and toward something that is much broader and has the potential for sweeping regional impact," said Dan Erikson, a Caribbean expert at the Inter-American Dialogue policy group in Washington.

"Raúl Castro is strongly interested in moving beyond an alliance built on personalities by creating sustainable, institutional arrangements, and this has helped to cement the Cuban-Venezuelan relationship," he said.

Oil Wealth

Venezuela, which is benefiting from high oil prices, is buying new rice harvesters and irrigation systems in central Cuba, upgrading fertilizer manufacturing and building new factories in the eastern city of Santiago [de Cuba].

The two countries have also signed some 30 joint ventures, most of which were sealed after Raúl Castro first stepped in for his ailing brother two years ago [in 2006]. Some are huge by Cuban standards.

A $5 billion petrochemical complex under construction around a renovated oil refinery in Cienfuegos, 150 miles (250 km) southeast of Havana, represents more direct investment than hundreds of Western businesses put into Cuba between 1995 and 2000.

There are an assortment of other oil-related ventures, from pipelines and refinery expansions to shipping and port renovations.

A nickel plant in eastern Holguín province is getting a $700 million upgrade and will ship its product to Venezuela to be processed into stainless steel by a joint venture in which Cuba has a 49 percent stake.

New ventures are also under way in telecommunications, fishing, agriculture, boat building, railways and cement.

The two countries' economic ties are cloaked in secrecy, but Cuban president Fidel Castro valued them at $7 billion per year just before he took ill in July 2006 and provisionally handed power to his brother.

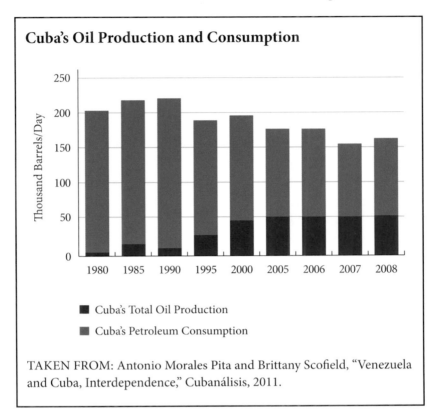

Cuba's Oil Production and Consumption

TAKEN FROM: Antonio Morales Pita and Brittany Scofield, "Venezuela and Cuba, Interdependence," Cubanálisis, 2011.

Too ill to return to power, Fidel Castro resigned in February and the National Assembly formally elected Raúl Castro president.

Most of the joint energy projects aim to serve Petrocaribe, a Venezuelan initiative that provides preferentially financed oil to 15 Caribbean and Central American countries.

For Cuba, its state-run economy worn down by inefficiency, 46 years of a U.S. trade embargo and dealt a severe blow by the collapse of its former Soviet benefactors [in the early 1990s], Venezuela's help has brought welcome improvements.

Daily life in Cuba remains difficult by Western standards, but there are fewer blackouts; subsidized buses are back on the roads; health clinics, schools, waterworks and highways are being upgraded and more housing built.

The danger, experts said, is [if] Cuba becomes as dependent on Venezuela as it did on the Soviet Union during the Cold War.

"For Cuba it is the best deal in town. However, it of course implies dangers, as Cuba becomes dependent on Chávez staying in power and remaining as generous as he is at present," said Cuba specialist Bert Hoffmann at the German Institute of Global [and] Area Studies in Hamburg.

| "Cuba's Communist regime seems finally to have achieved its goal of invading oil-rich Venezuela."

Many Venezuelans Resent Cuban Aid and Influence

The Economist

The Economist *is a weekly British news and business magazine. In the following viewpoint, it reports that Cuba and Venezuela are moving closer and closer together. The* Economist *says that Cuban officials may actually control health policy in key respects and that Cuban intelligence officials are heavily involved in Venezuelan security. Fidel Castro has said that Venezuela and Cuba are one nation, but, according to the* Economist, *an overwhelming majority of Venezuelans do not want their country to become more like Cuba.*

As you read, consider the following questions:

1. According to the *Economist*, who is Ramiro Valdés, and what may be his role in Venezuela?

2. Why does the *Economist* say that trade unions have complained about the Cubans in Venezuela?

3. What percentage of Venezuelans did not want their country to become more like Cuba, according to the *Economist*?

In a small fishing village on the Caribbean coast of Venezuela stands a plinth. Unveiled by government officials in 2006, it pays homage to the Cuban guerrillas sent by Fidel Castro in the 1960s to help subvert Venezuela's then recently restored democracy. Almost entirely bereft of popular support, the guerrilla campaign flopped. But four decades later, and after a decade of rule by Hugo Chávez, Cuba's Communist regime seems finally to have achieved its goal of invading oil-rich Venezuela—this time without firing a shot.

Cubans in Control

Earlier this month [February 2010] Ramiro Valdés, a veteran revolutionary who ranks number three in Cuba's ruling hierarchy and was twice its interior minister, arrived in Caracas, apparently for a long stay. Officially, Mr Valdés has come to head a commission set up by Mr Chávez to resolve Venezuela's acute electricity shortage. But he lacks expertise in this field, and Cuba is famous for 12-hour blackouts. Some members of Venezuela's opposition reckon that Mr Valdés, whose responsibilities at home include policing Cubans' access to the Internet, has come to help Mr Chávez step up repression ahead of a legislative election in September. Others believe he was sent to assess the gravity of the situation facing the Castro brothers' most important ally (Cuba depends on Mr Chávez for subsidised oil). He has been seen in meetings with Venezuelan military commanders.

Although by far the most senior, Mr Valdés is only one among many Cubans who have been deployed by Mr Chávez under bilateral agreements that took shape in 2003. As well as thousands of doctors staffing a community-health programme, they include people who are helping to run Venezuela's ports, telecommunications, police training, the issuing of identity documents and the business registry.

In 2005 Venezuela's government gave Cuba a contract to modernise its identity-card system. Since then, Cuban officials have been spotted in agencies such as immigration and passport control. A group of Cubans who recently fled Venezuela told a newspaper in Miami that they had bribed a Cuban official working in passport control at Caracas airport.

In some ministries, such as health and agriculture, Cuban advisers appear to wield more power than Venezuelan officials. The health ministry is often unable to provide statistics—on primary health care or epidemiology for instance—because the information is sent back to Havana instead. Mr Chávez seemed to acknowledge this last year when, by his own account, he learned that thousands of primary health care posts had been shut down only when Mr Castro told him so.

Venecuba

Coffee growers complain that in meetings with the government it is Bárbara Castillo, a former Cuban trade minister, who calls the shots. Ms Castillo, who was formally seconded to Venezuela four years ago, refuses requests for interviews.

Trade unions, particularly in the oil and construction industries, have complained of ill-treatment by the Cubans. No unions are allowed on Cuban-run building sites. In September last year, Froilán Barrios of the Confederation of Venezuelan Workers, which opposes the government, said that "oil and petrochemicals are completely penetrated by Cuban G2," the Castros' fearsomely efficient intelligence service. Oil workers planning a strike said they had been threatened by Cuban officials.

The new national police force and the army have both adopted policies inspired by Cuba. The chief adviser to the national police-training academy is a Cuban, and Venezuela's defence doctrine is based on Cuba's "war of all the people". Foreign officials who watch Venezuela closely say that Cuban agents occupy key posts in Venezuela's military intelligence agency, but these claims are impossible to verify.

Mr Chávez portrays Cuban help as socialist solidarity in the struggle against "the empire", as he calls the United States. When he was visiting Cuba in 2005, Fidel Castro said publicly to him that their two countries were "a single nation". "With one flag," added Mr Chávez, to which Mr Castro replied, "We are Venecubans." These views are not shared by Venezuelans. In a recent poll, 85% of respondents said they did not want their country to become like Cuba. Perhaps Mr Valdés will include that in his assessment.

| "*Canada could enhance its position and prestige in the hemisphere by standing up to the Americans on Cuba.*"

Canada Should Establish Closer Relations with Cuba

Peter McKenna

Peter McKenna is a professor of political science at the University of Prince Edward Island and the editor of the book Canada Looks South: In Search of an Americas Policy. *In the following viewpoint, he argues that Canada should seek closer ties with Cuba. He says that Canada should arrange high-level diplomatic visits with Cuba and should push back against America's Cuban embargo and anti-Cuba policy. McKenna says that Canada would improve its relations with Latin America if it would distance itself from America's Cuba policy.*

As you read, consider the following questions:

1. Who is Diane Ablonczy, and why does McKenna praise her?

2. What Florida state bill does McKenna say Canada should oppose, and why?

3. What does McKenna say Canada should do to show that it is standing up to Americans in regard to Cuba?

Following last weekend's [April 2012] Summit of the Americas in Cartagena, Colombia, [Canadian] Prime Minister Stephen Harper needs to seriously reassess his position on Cuba (which was not officially invited to the inter-American gathering) and reset the Canadian–Latin American relationship.

Huge Opportunities

Indeed, we can't on the one hand criticize the U.S. government for a failed Cuba policy (after 50 years of ineffective economic sanctions) and then side with the Americans on excluding Havana from the Americas summit process. Additionally, we should not forget that Cuba punches well above its weight within the wider region.

Notwithstanding recent comments by former Cuban president Fidel Castro, who castigated Harper for environmental damage caused by Alberta's oil sands and Canadian mining companies for exploiting struggling communities in many Latin American countries, the Canadian government should seek to strengthen its relationship with Havana. Minister of State for Foreign Affairs (Americas and Consular Services), Diane Ablonczy, has already done some important work in this area. She has properly recognized that there exist huge opportunities where both Canada and Cuba can work constructively together on a wide range of issue areas, including trade, tourism, energy and people-to-people contacts.

The next step is for Foreign Affairs Minister John Baird to undertake an official visit to Havana in the coming months. That, of course, would set the stage for a prime ministerial visit to Cuba—or a visit by a senior-ranking Cuban government official ([President] Raúl Castro?) to Ottawa in the near term.

But as former prime minister Jean Chrétien found out during his own April 1998 visit to Cuba, it makes no sense to press the Cubans hard on the human rights front or to attach certain conditions to a continued warming in bilateral relations. Yes, we should raise the issue of democratization and respect for political rights and freedoms, but if we hope to influence them here we should do so in a respectful and non-accusatory manner (and without preconditions).

Florida's Foreign Policy

Canada could also earn some diplomatic credit with its Cuban friends (and build stronger linkages with the Argentines, Brazilians and Mexicans) by pushing U.S. president Barack Obama on an anti-Cuba bill passed by the Florida state legislature in March [2012]. Harper should firmly ask Obama if there is any way that this counterproductive bill can be quashed. The offending legislation was sponsored by Miami Republican lawmakers determined to punish the Cubans by restricting state and local governments from signing procurement contracts with any companies that do business with Cuba and Syria. Both countries still remain on the U.S. State Department's list of state sponsors of terrorism.

The point here is not only to prevent Florida taxpayers from supporting companies that have commercial relations with Havana, but to compel those same companies from operating and investing in Cuba. In a word: It's about "internationalizing" the U.S. economic embargo against Cuba—which has always been seen in Washington as the key instrument for removing the Castros from power.

Clearly, if this bill is signed into law by Florida governor Rick Scott, it could have negative repercussions for Canadian companies bidding on contracts in the Sunshine State.

But the constitutionality of such a bill is seriously in doubt, since only the federal government (and Congress) in Washington has the legislative competence to conduct foreign policy

Canada vs. America on Cuba

In 1996 a private member's bill was introduced into the Canadian Parliament to allow descendants of the United Empire Loyalists to claim compensation for the land confiscated by the United States government after the American Revolution in 1776. The Godfrey-Milliken Bill, though never passed, was written in retaliation for an American measure designed to hamper other countries from investing in Cuba. This measure, the Cuban Liberty and Democratic Solidarity (*Libertad*) Act, commonly known as the Helms-Burton Act [after sponsors Senator Jesse Helms and Representative Dan Burton], outraged Canadians because they interpreted it as Washington trying to dictate Canadian policy. Outrage was directed north as well. U.S. senator Jesse Helms compared Canada's relationship with Cuba to Britain's appeasement of Hitler at Munich. He declared that Canadians should 'be ashamed of themselves.' A Canadian member of Parliament shot back by calling the United States a 'bully.' The minister of foreign affairs, Lloyd Axworthy, remarked that 'Helms-Burton is bad legislation.'

Lana Wylie,
Perceptions of Cuba: Canadian and
American Policies in Comparative Perspective.
Toronto: University of Toronto Press, 2010.

(and impose sanctions). And it is well established that state and local governments are constitutionally prohibited from setting policy that conflicts with federal lawmaking responsibilities. A similar law in Massachusetts—which sought to limit state businesses from dealing with companies inking commercial deals with rights-abusing Burma—was struck down by the U.S. Supreme Court in 2000.

Canada could enhance its position and prestige in the hemisphere by standing up to the Americans on Cuba. Accordingly, it should seek Cuba's presence at the next Americas summit, should there be one.

While most of what Fidel Castro said in early April can be ignored, he was right about highlighting the constructive engagement approach of former Canadian prime ministers Pierre Trudeau and Jean Chrétien toward Cuba. Indeed, we need to jettison ideologically tinged rhetoric and focus on positive interaction, cooperative dialogue and commercial exchange.

To be sure, one of the keys to Canada opening up the door to wider and deeper relations with the Americas has to involve Cuba. Taking up the question of Cuba's importance in the region is a good place for Stephen Harper to begin.

> "It seems strange . . . that Cuba, so long a focus of fascination for many Canadians, rarely seems to register on our human rights radar."

Canada Should Focus on Human Rights in Cuba

John Geddes

John Geddes is a journalist who writes on politics and policy for Maclean's. In the following viewpoint, he argues that Canada should be more engaged with the problem of human rights abuses in Cuba. He points out that a dissident Cuban individual on a hunger strike died protesting the regime, and he also highlights Cuba's practice of imprisoning journalists and those who speak out against the regime. He argues that Canada sends a large number of tourists to Cuba each year and that such close ties require Canada to speak out against Cuban abuses.

As you read, consider the following questions:

1. Who are Orlando Zapata Tamayo and Guillermo Farinas Hernandez, and why are they important, according to Geddes?

2. Why does Geddes say that Canadians know Cuba better than anybody?

3. According to Peter Kent, what is Canada's position on human rights in Cuba?

When Canadians concern themselves with human rights abuses these days—if they do at all—their minds tend to turn to jailed Chinese dissidents, to detainees in Afghan prisons, and maybe to Omar Khadr, the young Canadian citizen still held by the U.S. at Guantánamo Bay.

Cuban Repression

There's good reason to worry about any or all of these issues. But it seems strange to me that Cuba, so long a focus of fascination for many Canadians, rarely seems to register on our human rights radar. It should, and maybe it soon will.

It's taken one dissident Cuban hunger-striker's death to attract a bit of the world's attention, and another's sickness to hold it. Orlando Zapata Tamayo died in February [2010] and Guillermo Farinas Hernandez has been hospitalized since March.

The hunger strikes create a contentious backdrop for the planned visit of the Vatican's foreign minister, Archbishop Dominique Mamberti, to Havana next month. The Catholic Church is increasingly active in Cuba, as its old Communist regime struggles to counter the recent uptick in international attention to the way it crushes dissent and silences debate.

Earlier this month, PEN Canada, represented by novelist Yann Martel, among others, joined an international "Freedom to Write in the Americas" campaign. Although PEN takes aim at the repression writers face in other Latin American countries too, it's hard to miss the fact that of 30 writers imprisoned for their work in the Western Hemisphere, 26 are in Cuba.

Canadians should be at the forefront of protesting that outrage. After all, we know Cuba better than just about anybody: Canada is Cuba's largest source of tourists, with 818,000 of us traveling there in 2008, nearly 35 per cent of all visitors to the island. That's a lot of contact. It shouldn't come without a sense of obligation to speak out and exert pressure.

Some argue that talking too loudly about Cuba's systematic violation of its citizens' human rights is counterproductive. John Keenan, writing in the *Guardian* today, reports that two British professors, commenting on the release of PEN's report "Free Expression in Cuba," "called for journalists to tread lightly when highlighting human rights abuses on the island, for fear of strengthening the Castro regime's argument that the sovereignty of the island is under siege."

It's hard to accept that cautious approach when dissidents are starving themselves to death for the right to free expression. And when Human Rights Watch has recently documented and reported on the extent of government repression in Cuba, painting a disturbing picture in [a] gripping *New York Review of Books* essay.

Proximity Matters

For Canadians, I think, proximity matters. PEN reports that "only China, Iran and Burma imprison more writers [than Cuba does] for exercising their right to freedom of expression." But China, Iran and Burma are a long way off for most Canadians, whereas Cuba is one of our favourite destinations for a week of sun and sand.

On Feb. 25, Foreign Affairs Minister Lawrence Cannon issued a statement decrying the death two days earlier of Orlando Zapata Tamayo. We can only hope that, behind the scenes, the Canadian government is doing all it can, and not simply waiting for the next dissident to die.

UPDATE:

This comes by e-mail from the office of Peter Kent, the minister of state of foreign affairs responsible for the Americas:

"Canada's position is clear: We support a free and democratic future for Cuba in which human rights and the rule of law are an everyday reality. In keeping with these universal values, the government of Canada calls upon Cuba to release all political prisoners immediately. We strongly urge Cuba to tolerate freedom of expression and other basic human rights. In the case of Guillermo Farinas Hernandez, we are monitoring the situation closely and receiving updates about his health from knowledgeable channels." (Kent's office notes that Farinas, a dissident journalist, is not a political prisoner. Farinas began his hunger strike to demand the release of prisoners at his home.)

Periodical and Internet Sources Bibliography

The following articles have been selected to supplement the diverse views presented in this chapter.

BBC News	"Russia to Drill for Oil Off Cuba," July 29, 2009. http://news.bbc.co.uk.
Mike Blanchfield	"Canada Welcomes Cuban Reforms on Eve of Tour by Harper's Latin America Minister," *Canadian Business*, January 8, 2012.
Sergey Borisov	"ROAR: 'Cuba May Occupy a New Place in World Architecture,'" RT, February 12, 2010. http://rt.com.
Marce Cameron	"Venezuela and Cuba: One Revolution," *Direct Action*, August 2009.
Economist	"Cuba and Venezuela: If Hugo Goes," July 7, 2011.
Humberto Fontova	"Hezbollah Opens Base in Cuba," *FrontPage*, September 6, 2011.
Jeff Franks	"Iranian Leader Says Cuba, Iran Think Alike," Reuters, January 12, 2012. www.reuters.com.
Nikolas Kozloff	"How Will Venezuela's Vote Affect Ties with Cuba?," Al Jazeera, March 28, 2012. www.aljazeera.com.
Peter McKenna	"Canada and the Americas: What About Cuba?," *Tico Times* (Central America), August 11, 2011.
Michael Schwirtz	"Russia and Cuba Take Steps to Revive a Bond," *New York Times*, January 30, 2009.
Juan O. Tamayo	"Fiber-Optic Cable Benefiting Only Cuban Government," *Miami Herald*, May 25, 2012.

CHAPTER 3

What Is the Relationship Between Cuba Policy and US Domestic Politics?

Chapter Preface

Cuban Americans have long played a major role in US politics. One recent example is Marco Rubio, who is currently US senator for Florida.

On his website, Rubio says that his parents left Cuba in 1956, a few years before the Cuban revolution, and that they were unable to return because of Fidel Castro's Communist regime. Like many children of Cuban émigrés, he was born in Miami. According to a January 18, 2012, article by John Avlon at the Daily Beast, his father worked as a bartender and his mother at the night shift at Walmart. Coming out of this working-class background, Rubio became the first Cuban American speaker of the Florida state House of Representatives. In 2010 he beat popular incumbent governor Republican Charlie Crist in a difficult three-way battle for the Florida Senate seat, making him one of the first people of his generation to become a nationally influential politician.

The Cuban American community has long been Republican and conservative, and Rubio follows in that tradition. In his website biography, he expresses support for a balanced budget amendment to the Constitution and argues for repealing Democratic president Barack Obama's health care initiative, the Patient Protection and Affordable Care Act. On Cuba policy, Rubio has taken a hard line, arguing that there should be no US change to the embargo against Cuba unless the Communist government moves toward democratization, according to a February 2011 blog post by Roque Planas.

One of Rubio's best-known legislative initiatives was an effort to allow the children of some undocumented immigrants to stay in the United States to pursue military careers or college. The bill had only limited support among Republicans. It was thought, however, that Mitt Romney, the 2012 Republican presidential candidate, might embrace it in hopes of improving his standing with Hispanic voters, according to Richard Cowan in a June 17, 2012, report on *Huffington Post*. However, in 2012 Barack Obama made a unilateral executive decision to stop deportations of young undocumented immigrants, effectively stealing the heart of Rubio's bill and killing its already low chances of passing.

Rubio remains, however, a rising star in the Republican Party and had been widely discussed as a vice-presidential possibility in 2012. Speculation was in part because Rubio is from Florida, a very large state that is generally considered up for grabs in presidential elections. His Cuban heritage was also a plus, as Mike Allison wrote in a May 23, 2012, article for Al Jazeera. Again, Republicans are losing ground with Hispanic voters because of their strong anti-immigration stance. Rubio is part of one of the few Hispanic constituencies—Cuban Americans—who consistently vote Republican. He would be the first Latino on a presidential ticket and might help the Republican candidate in states like Colorado, New Mexico, and Nevada, where Rubio spent his early years, as well as in Florida.

Although Rubio was not chosen as the vice-presidential nominee, he seems to have a long and promising political career ahead of him. He demonstrates the continuing domestic political importance of Cuban Americans as well as the long-standing and ongoing links between Cuba and the United States. The viewpoints in the following chapter explore those links further by discussing other ways in which Cuban Americans, along with the issue of Cuba policy, has influenced US domestic politics.

"Cuban intelligence has successfully compromised every major US military operation since the 1983 invasion of Grenada."

Cuba Is a Security Threat to the United States

James M. Roberts

James M. Roberts is research fellow for economic freedom and growth at the Heritage Foundation. In the following viewpoint, he argues that Cuba is a serious threat to US national security. He argues that Cuba spreads anti-Americanism throughout Latin America and supports anti-American regimes like Hugo Chávez's in Venezuela. Roberts also says that Cuba's intelligence service spies on American activities and sells the resulting information to other nations, compromising US military operations and security. Roberts says that the United States should work to counter Cuban intelligence activities and to promote democracy in Cuba.

As you read, consider the following questions:

1. What is the DI, and why does Roberts argue that it is dangerous?

2. According to Roberts, what is the intelligence relationship between Cuba and China?

3. What is one recommendation that Roberts makes to the George W. Bush administration about security in relation to Cuba?

On September 17, [2007] U.S. Secretary of Commerce Carlos M. Gutierrez launched the 2007–2008 Heritage Foundation series "Cuba at the Crossroads," which explores the choices Cuba faces after the end of Fidel Castro's 50-year reign. The next event in the series will focus on the threat that Cuba currently poses to U.S. national security through its activities in Latin America, intelligence operations, and relations with U.S. enemies.

Cuba at the Crossroads will provide a series of perspectives to support U.S. government planning for the transition that will occur in Cuba after the (perhaps imminent) death of Fidel Castro.

After 50 years of tyranny, will Cubans finally be free to build a market-based democracy? Or will the Castro regime's apparatchiks cling to control of Castro's totalitarian machinery? What will be the role of Venezuelan dictator and Castro protégé Hugo Chávez? Will the Cuban people be forced to endure 50 more years of life in a cruel command-economy police state?

Over the next few months, leaders from Congress, the executive branch, academia, and the media will come to Heritage to lead focused discussions on the potential role of the United States in shaping post-Castro Cuba, the future of U.S.-Cuba relations, and the role a newly democratic Cuba might play in the hemisphere.

Cuba's Threat

The next event will feature a discussion of the many ways that Castro's Cuba threatens U.S. national security. A number of security issues stand out:

A Cuban Spy

Ana Belen Montes ... recently marked her fiftieth birthday at a federal penitentiary in southern Texas.... In 1985, she won a coveted job as an analyst with the Defense Intelligence Agency (DIA), the military intelligence arm of the Pentagon.... Montes moved steadily up the hierarchy, ... gaining greater and greater levels of access to the United States' most classified secrets. Initially focused on the Latin American region, Montes began to specialize in Cuban affairs. In 1992, she was detailed exclusively to Cuba, and by the end of the decade she was the DIA's most senior-level analyst for Cuba. In 2001, she won a highly competitive National Intelligence Council fellowship....

But Montes never received her promised fellowship. In early 2001, her seemingly impeccable career started to unravel when an internal investigation about a possible Cuban spy in the U.S. security apparatus began to focus on Montes as the chief suspect. By May, the FBI was regularly tailing Montes, and it gathered enough information to file an indictment against her. [After the September 11, 2001 terrorist attacks] the decision was made that it was too risky to leave Montes at large.... On the morning of September 20, 2001, Montes was ... taken into federal custody. On the day of her arrest, a spokesperson for the FBI's Washington field office declared, "This has been a very important investigation, because it does show our national defense information is still being targeted by the Cuban intelligence service." In fact, Montes had been recruited as a Cuban spy even before she joined the Pentagon during the [Ronald] Reagan administration, and her espionage activities reached back sixteen years.

Daniel P. Erikson,
The Cuba Wars: Fidel Castro, the United States,
and the Next Revolution, *2008.*

- Cuba is aggressively spreading anti-Americanism throughout Latin America and is deeply involved in backing and advising the increasingly totalitarian and virulently anti-U.S. regime of Venezuelan dictator-president Hugo Chávez.

- Since Raúl Castro took the reins as acting head of state in 2006, Cuban intelligence services have intensified their targeting of the U.S. Since 9/11 [referring to the terrorist attacks of September 11, 2001], however, U.S. intelligence agencies have reduced the priority assigned to Cuba.

- Cuba's Directorate of Intelligence (DI) is among the top six intelligence services in the world. Thirty-five of its intelligence officers or agents have been identified operating in the U.S. and neutralized between 1996 and 2003. This is strong evidence of DI's aggressiveness and hostility toward the U.S.

- Cuba traffics in intelligence. U.S. intelligence secrets collected by Cuba have been sold to or bartered with Russia, China, North Korea, Iran, and other enemies of the United States. China is known to have had intelligence personnel posted to the Cuban Signals Intelligence (SIGINT) site at Bejucal since 2001, and Russia continues to receive Cuban SIGINT information. Additionally, many Cuban intelligence agents and security police are advising Hugo Chávez in Venezuela.

- Cuban intelligence has successfully compromised every major U.S. military operation since the 1983 invasion of Grenada and has provided America's enemies with forewarning of impending U.S. operations.

- Beijing is busy working to improve Cuban Signals Intelligence and electronic warfare facilities, which had languished after the fall of the Soviet Union, integrating them into China's own global satellite network. Mary O'Grady of the *Wall Street Journal* has noted that this means the Chinese army, at a cyber-warfare complex 20 miles south of Havana, can now monitor phone conversations and Internet transmissions in America.

Recommendations for the George W. Bush Administration and Congress

- The [George W.] Bush administration should raise the priority of Cuba at all U.S. defense and intelligence agencies.

- The Bush administration should increase funding for efforts by these agencies to counter the Cuban intelligence threat as the post-Castro transition approaches.

- Congress should hold hearings on ways that current threats to U.S. national security can be eliminated and market-based democracy can be promoted in post-Castro Cuba.

"Cuba is a sponsor of terrorism, in other words, because it is critical of America's war on terrorism. By this definition, many of America's elected officials are sponsors of terrorism."

Don't Lump Cuba with Iran on US Terror List

Jeffrey Goldberg

Jeffrey Goldberg is a columnist for Bloomberg and a national correspondent for the Atlantic. *In the following viewpoint, he argues that Cuba has done nothing to merit inclusion on the State Department's list of state sponsors of terrorism. The State Department accuses Cuba of criticizing US antiterrorism policy, which Goldberg says is hardly a terrorist act. Goldberg argues that the state sponsors of terrorism list actually just lists regimes that the United States has decided to despise, for various political reasons that may or may not have anything to do with terrorism. He concludes that the list is misleading and damages US foreign policy.*

As you read, consider the following questions:

1. According to Goldberg, what evidence is there that Pakistan is a state supporter of terrorism?

2. How has Cuba cooperated with the United States on airport security, according to Goldberg?

3. What does Goldberg say are the consequences of being placed on the US state sponsors of terrorism list?

Here is some of what we know about the disorderly, nuclear-armed state of Pakistan: We know that the world's most notorious terrorist, Osama bin Laden, found refuge there for several years. We know that bin Laden's organization, al Qaeda, has moved its headquarters to Pakistan's sovereign territory.

We know that Lashkar-e-Taiba, the terrorist group that was responsible for devastating attacks in Mumbai in 2008, maintains a 200-acre campus near Lahore. And we know that Pakistan's intelligence agency has given direct support to terrorist groups, including Lashkar and the Haqqani Network, which is responsible for the deaths of U.S. soldiers in Afghanistan.

Pakistan, it seems, would be a natural candidate for inclusion on the "state sponsors of terrorism" list that the U.S. State Department produces each year.

But it isn't on the list.

Here is some of what we know about Cuba. Cuba is an impoverished autocracy. Its superannuated leaders are gradually opening their country's economy. Cuba is reducing the size of its military, it has condemned al Qaeda and it poses no national security threat to the U.S. No serious intelligence analyst believes that Cuba is still funding or arming foreign insurgencies.

But Cuba is on the list. So what, exactly, has it done to merit inclusion?

Criticism Equals Terrorism

According to the State Department's 2010 report on state sponsors of terrorism, "Cuba continued to denounce U.S.

counterterrorism efforts throughout the world, portraying them as a pretext to extend U.S. influence and power."

Cuba is a sponsor of terrorism, in other words, because it is critical of America's war on terrorism. By this definition, many of America's elected officials are sponsors of terrorism.

The report goes on, "Cuba has been used as a transit point by third-country nationals looking to enter illegally into the United States." By this definition, Canada is also a sponsor of terrorism.

And what are the Cubans doing about this problem? "The government of Cuba is aware of the border integrity and transnational security concerns posed by such transit and investigated third-country migrant smuggling and related criminal activities."

Oh, and by the way, the Cubans also "allowed representatives of the Transportation Security Administration to conduct a series of airport security visits throughout the island." A very clever co-optation by a terrorist state, apparently.

The department's 2009 report acknowledged that Cuba "publicly condemned acts of terrorism by al-Qa'ida and its affiliates," but still made the point that the government in Havana was "critical of the U.S. approach to combating international terrorism."

And it detailed another of Cuba's treacheries: "The government of Cuba has long assisted members of the Revolutionary Armed Forces of Colombia (FARC), the National Liberation Army of Colombia (ELN), and Spain's Basque and Freedom (ETA) organization, some having arrived in Cuba in connection with peace negotiations with the governments of Colombia and Spain."

I asked Julia E. Sweig, the Latin America expert at the Council on Foreign Relations, what to make of this claim. She said, "Cuba hosted peace talks at the request of a succession of

Colombian governments. But Norway hosted the PLO during the run-up to the Oslo peace process. Did this make Norway a state sponsor of terror?"

Cuba is a one-party state, of course, and its people deserve to be free. Just last week, Cuba hosted the president of a terrorist state, Iran. This is perfidious, but it doesn't make Cuba a state sponsor of terrorism.

Harsh Consequences

The State Department's list has consequences. Harsh sanctions automatically accompany the designation of a country as a sponsor of terrorism. And it is used as a guide by U.S. allies when they formulate foreign policy.

In total, there are four countries listed. Syria and Iran are two. This makes sense to me. But the final country is Sudan. Here is what the State Department's most recent report on Sudan says about its dastardly activities: "Sudan remained a cooperative partner in global counterterrorism efforts against al-Qa'ida (AQ) in 2010."

Come again? Sudan cooperates in American antiterrorism activities? The report goes on, "During the past year, the government of Sudan worked actively to counter AQ operations that posed a potential threat to U.S. interests and personnel in Sudan. Sudanese officials have indicated that they viewed continued cooperation with the United States as important and recognized the potential benefits of U.S. training and information sharing."

Sudan isn't ruled by good or generous people, and its government violates the rights of its citizens in diverse ways, but how could it be a state sponsor of terrorism when the State Department labels it an ally in fighting terrorists?

President Barack Obama's administration is aware of the flaws in this list. One senior administration official acknowledged to me that some of its features are absurd. But he argued that including a country draws attention to its wrongdoing and makes other nations think twice about doing business with it.

In reality, though, the list is hopelessly corrupted by politics. If it was an exercise in analytical honesty, Cuba would be the first country removed. But no administration would risk the wrath of the Cuba lobby in Washington by doing so. This is to our detriment, as much as it is to Cuba's.

So why have a list at all? I wouldn't argue for Pakistan's inclusion, even though elements of the Pakistani government support terrorism, because the U.S. shouldn't handcuff itself in dealing with complicated and dangerous countries. If the list is to remain, it should at least be renamed: The State Department's List of Countries That, for One Reason or Another, We Have Decided to Despise.

It's a mouthful, but at least it reflects reality.

| "*Younger Cubans are brandishing a more independent outlook.*"

Cuban Americans May Be Moving Away from the Republican Party

Alex Leary

Alex Leary is a staff writer for the Tampa Bay Times *focusing on national politics. In the following viewpoint, he reports that the Cuban American community is less reliably Republican than it once was. He attributes this to a generational shift; older Cuban exiles who fled the island in the sixties because of the revolution are still very Republican, but their children are more independent. Leary says that the trend is likely to continue, and that as older Cubans die and younger ones come to voting age, the Republican Party will be able to rely less and less on a solid Cuban vote in Florida.*

As you read, consider the following questions:

1. According to Leary, what percentage of the Cuban vote did Barack Obama get in Florida in 2008, and how did this compare to John McCain?

2. Who are the Mariel boatlift immigrants, and how did they affect Cuban voting patterns, according to Leary?

3. How does Leary say that immigration policy may influence Cuban voters?

Anton Fajardo voted for John McCain in 2008 [in the U.S. presidential election] but is now for Barack Obama.

Alex Toledo backed Obama yet likes Ron Paul.

Juan Morales also voted for Obama, and thinks he will again, but is keeping an open mind.

Three perspectives on the 2012 election with a common tie: Fajardo, Toledo and Morales are in their early 30s and of Cuban descent. Together they represent an ideological shift that is altering Florida's political landscape and may help decide the presidency.

Young Cubans

A couple of generations removed from the exile experience of the 1960s [when many Cubans fled to Florida after the Cuban revolution led by Fidel Castro], which created lockstep allegiance to the strongly anti-Communist GOP [referring to the Republican Party], younger Cubans are brandishing a more independent outlook.

"Any Cuban I know who is over 45 years will vote Republican no matter what," Fajardo, 32, said over the lunchtime commotion of Miami Beach's Lincoln Road. "I think my peers will vote as I do, whoever they think is the best candidate."

The [2012] race between Obama and Mitt Romney, the presumptive GOP nominee, is expected to be a repeat of Florida's 2008 election, in which Obama's victory with less than 3 percent of the vote proved that no advantage or weakness among 1.2 million Cuban-American residents can be overlooked.

Obama captured 35 percent of the Cuban-American vote four years ago, more than any Democrat since Bill Clinton in

1996 and 65 percent of support from voters ages 18 to 29. McCain took 66 percent of the vote from Cubans ages 50 to 64 and 79 percent from those 65 to 74.

"My dad's a die-hard Republican. He always brings it up saying, 'You voted for Obama and the situation we're in is all your fault,'" said Toledo, 32, who manages the interactive department at a marketing firm in Miami Beach.

That Toledo is leaning toward long shot Paul—Obama, he said, did not deliver the change he promised—is a sign the president has work to do among a group that harbors some of the same disillusionment as other young voters.

Falling Republican Support

It used to be enough for Republican politicians to sweep in to Miami, sip Cuban coffee at Versailles restaurant and hammer on Fidel Castro to seal the Cuban vote that makes up about 70 percent of the Republican electorate in Miami-Dade [County].

But the younger generation is less motivated by those politics, having assimilated into mainstream U.S. culture.

"I grew up thinking I was Republican and it wasn't until I started asking questions and not getting answers besides, 'Oh because [President John F.] Kennedy betrayed us,' that I started to change," said Aimee Valera, referring to the botched Bay of Pigs invasion a half century ago [in April 1961]. Valera, who was born in Cuba, sought citizenship so she could vote for Obama and is volunteering for his campaign. She's trying to convert her sister, who favors Republicans but "is leaning toward the Democratic side" because of women's issues, Valera said.

The change is also driven by the introduction of Mariel boatlift immigrants into the voting class. Fleeing Cuba en masse in 1980, the refugees were driven more by economic than political reasons. Along with more recent arrivals, they tend to be less against the trade embargo and more in favor of increased travel with Cuba.

Political strategists in Miami caution against drawing too strong a connection to U.S. policy and fading allegiances, but for various reasons, overall GOP support among Cuban-Americans has dropped by nearly 20 percent . . . since 2000.

Republicans, who face much broader concerns over attracting non-Cuban Hispanics, expect the economy will reverse the trend and pledge an aggressive outreach program in South Florida. Obama's also not the cool new guy, either.

"Obama was a very unique candidate but this is a whole new ball game," said Bettina Inclan, director of Hispanic outreach for the Republican National Committee. "I think there's no more emotional issue when you can't figure out how to pay your bills and achieve the American Dream."

Others are unsure.

"If we would have had this conversation a year ago, I would have said the economy is going to force Cubans back," said Darío Moreno, a pollster and political science professor at Florida International University [FIU]. But he said the GOP presidential debates renewed anti-immigration rhetoric.

While Cubans enjoy protected status under U.S. law, Moreno said, they are no less sensitive to the debate: "At some point Republicans sound not anti-immigration but anti-Hispanic."

When they register to vote, Hispanics are turning to the Democratic Party or to no party affiliation, a sign the GOP's hard-line stance is turning them off.

Who Will Vote?

J.C. Planas, a former Republican state lawmaker who is Cuban-American, thinks the economy will help turn back Obama's

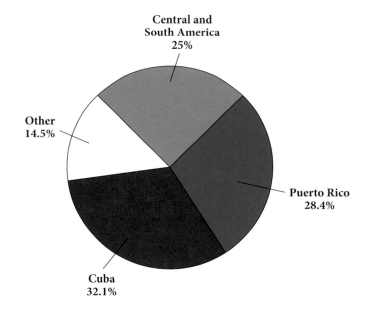

Country of Origin of Registered Hispanic Voters in Florida

Central and
South America
25%

Other
14.5%

Puerto Rico
28.4%

Cuba
32.1%

TAKEN FROM: Laura Wides-Munoz, "Latino Vote 2012: In Florida, the Focus Is on the Cuban-American Vote," *Huffington Post*, January 29, 2012. www.huffingtonpost.com.

advantage. But he said his party has a branding problem, allowing itself to become symbolic of rigid social views on gay rights and abortion, for example, and should focus on economic and education issues.

"With Republicans, it's all about fear," said Aliette Carolan, 34, a lawyer in Miami, who is the daughter of Cuban exiles and voted for Obama. She said despite comparisons of the president's health care plan to socialism, it's popular among her peers. (Polling conducted by FIU bears this out.)

"It's not socialism," Carolan said. "It's about having a social conscience. It's about time the government stepped up and did something about health care in this country."

Carolan said she thinks younger Cubans will stick with Obama "not because they're so pleased with him but because Republicans have not presented anybody who is in any way better."

Older Cubans are still highly reliable Republicans, and they consistently turn out to vote.

Voter registration among Cubans who arrived during and after the 1980 Mariel boatlift is lower, said Vanessa Lopez, research associate at the Institute for Cuban and Cuban-American studies at the University of Miami. "The trick will be," she said, "as with all young people, is to get them out to vote."

Romney has in his camp some of the most prominent Cuban-American elected officials in South Florida, chiefly U.S. Sen. Marco Rubio, who turns 41 this month [May 2012]. While the shift may not be dramatic—Cuban-American members of Congress from South Florida have withstood Democratic challenges in recent elections—it is perceptible and expected to widen over the next decade as '60s exiles die off, forcing Republicans to expand their platform. "I think that's a good thing for our republic that the parties can't take any voters for granted and are going to have to earn people's support," Rubio said.

| "Cuban American voters' strict allegiance to the GOP ... will likely fade only gradually with time."

Cuban American Voters Continue to Support Republican Candidates

Benjamin G. Bishin and Casey A. Klofstad

Benjamin G. Bishin is associate professor of political science at the University of California, Riverside. Casey A. Klofstad is associate professor of political science at the University of Miami. In the following viewpoint, they report that Cubans who immigrated to the United States since 1980 and the Mariel boatlift refugees are less likely to support Republican candidates. However, the authors say, the post-Mariel immigrants are also poorer and less politically engaged, meaning that they have trouble paying for citizenship and tend to vote at low rates. As a result, pre-Mariel Cubans still dominate the electorate. According to the authors, Cuban voting patterns will change, but it will happen very slowly.

Benjamin G. Bishin and Casey A. Klofstad, "The Political Incorporation of Cuban Americans: Why Won't Little Havana Turn Blue?," *Political Research Quarterly*, vol. 20, no. 10, September 30, 2011, pp. 1–4, 8, 10–12. Copyright © 2011 by Sage Publications.

As you read, consider the following questions:

1. Before 1959, where was the Cuban American immigrant population concentrated, according to the authors?

2. According to the authors, how has the US attitude toward new immigrants changed since the 1960s?

3. According to the authors, what does an oft-repeated joke in Miami say is the Democrats' best hope for making inroads into the Cuban American community?

This [viewpoint] examines the political implications of the changing demographics of the Cuban American community. Over the past decade, pundits have predicted a massive shift in Cuban American voting behavior owing to demographic changes in the community. The authors find evidence that the attitudes of Cuban Americans have undergone significant changes, driven largely by the increased number of post-Mariel (1980) immigrants. The authors also find, however, that these dramatic changes have not yet been reflected at the ballot box, nor are they likely to be soon, owing to the slow process of immigrant political incorporation.

As the largest and fastest-growing ethnic group in the United States, scholars have increasingly come to recognize the important role that Latinos play in American politics. Between 1990 and 2008, the Latino population increased from 9 percent to 15.1 percent, and is expected to reach approximately 18 percent of the U.S. population by 2020. Even more importantly, Latinos are concentrated in some of the most competitive states (e.g., Florida, New Mexico), and their continued growth is expected to make other states more competitive in the near future (e.g., Texas).

The Exceptional Case of Cubans

Within this growing community, Cuban Americans are an exceptional case. Despite sharing similar cultural, social, religious, and linguistic backgrounds, Cuban Americans are distinctive among Latinos in their staunch support for the Republican Party. Cuban Americans routinely vote for Republican presidential candidates at rates exceeding 65 percent, turn out to vote at very high rates compared to other Latinos, and are disproportionately concentrated in Florida, arguably the most important presidential battleground state.

Having observed dramatic demographic changes in the Cuban community over the past decade, during each of the last two presidential campaigns scholars and pundits have predicted that Cuban Americans would abruptly turn and vote Democratic. By the year 2000, for instance, the community was about equally split between immigrants who arrived before and after the Mariel boatlift of 1980 [in which thousands of Cubans fled economic conditions on the island with the Cuban government's approval]. Unlike earlier political refugees, post-1980 immigrants tend to be economic refugees who lack the anti-Castro [referring to Cuban leader Fidel Castro] fervor that characterizes earlier émigrés' political views. Consequently, their ties to contemporary Cuba are much stronger, and they tend to hold more moderate political preferences, especially on questions of U.S. foreign policy toward Cuba.

Predictions of dramatic change in the attitudes and behavior of the Cuban American electorate are grounded in a distinguished literature on voting behavior that holds that social-psychological attachments like partisanship and predispositions toward key actors and about central issues strongly influence vote choice. From this perspective, the changing demographics that are occurring portend potentially dramatic change in voting patterns due to the increased numbers of post-Mariel immigrants and native-born Cuban Americans who are creating an electorate that is less staunchly Republican and less fiercely anti-Castro.

Cubans Remain Republican

While the logic of rapid change to Cuban Americans' vote choice is theoretically compelling, recent elections have evinced little support for the claim that the Cuban American electorate is becoming more progressive. The electorate's continued strong support for the GOP [referring to the Republican Party] is perhaps most clearly seen by examining Cuban American support for Republican presidential candidates. . . .

While the 2008 election saw the continuation of a trend of decreased support for the GOP among Cuban Americans since 2000, [Republican candidate] John McCain still garnered about 64 percent of the vote, a figure better than the 60.5 percent obtained by Bob Dole in 1996. Moreover, when one considers the extraordinary circumstances of the Elián González affair,[1] the 2000 election seems likely to represent a high-water mark for Cuban American support of Republicans. Given this context, the pattern is difficult to identify, but to the extent that a decline is occurring, it appears more gradual than sharp.

While these results run contrary both to pundits' prognostications and expectations of voting behavior studies, they are much more consistent with the implications of decades of research on political incorporation [of immigrant communities]. Research shows that political incorporation tends to occur gradually as an individual's resources, English fluency, age, education, generations in the United States, and most importantly, the amount of time a person has been in the United States all develop relatively slowly overtime. Consequently, the predictions of the research on political incorporation contradict the expectations implied by traditional accounts of voting behavior, which seldom account for immigrants.

---

1. Elián González was a young Cuban boy living with relatives in Miami. His father in Cuba successfully worked to have his son returned to him. The issue was very controversial in the Cuban American community.

This [viewpoint] examines the attitudes and behavior of Cuban Americans in light of the large demographic changes that have occurred over the past thirty years and is motivated by a simple question: Why do Cuban Americans still over-whelmingly support Republican candidates at the ballot box? Our results suggest that contrary to both pundits' predictions and the expectations of traditional models of voting behavior, Cuban Americans' behavior is better explained by research on political incorporation. As the foreign-born population consti-tutes a large and growing proportion of the U.S. popula-tion—in 2009, 12.5 percent of residents were foreign born, up from 4.7 percent in 1970—theories of incorporation have be-come increasingly important to understanding American po-litical behavior.

Our assessment of Cuban American voting behavior be-gins with a description of recent changes in the makeup and attitudes of the Cuban American community. We then offer an explanation for why Cuban Americans' voting behavior has not changed despite these shifts. Specifically, we argue that owing to their differing socializing experiences, those who im-migrated after the Mariel boatlift of 1980 tend to hold differ-ent attitudes than those who immigrated before. Moreover, consistent with the literature on political incorporation, post-Mariel immigrants' relatively low socioeconomic status, and the differing incentives provided by the U.S. government at the time of their arrival, leads to their dramatic underrepre-sentation in the voting electorate relative to pre-Mariel immi-grants. The differences in attitudes that map from the two dif-ferent immigration experiences to contemporary behavior both explain why Little Havana [referring to South Florida] refuses to turn blue and illustrate how the political incorpora-tion of Cuban immigrants has been influenced by traditional explanations of voting behavior (e.g., individual resources) as well as the institutional contexts that they left in Cuba and to which they arrived in the United States.

Change in the Cuban American Community

Over the past thirty years, the makeup of the Cuban American community has undergone a striking change. Before 1959, few Cuban Americans lived in South Florida as Tampa, Florida, and Union City, New Jersey, were the primary destinations for Cuban immigrants. Following the overthrow of the Batista government [referring to the rule of Fulgencio Batista], however, South Florida became the primary destination for Cuban immigrants such that by 2000, 58.9 percent of the approximately 1.3 million Cuban Americans living in the United States resided in Miami-Dade (656,751), Broward (53,150), or Palm Beach (26,157) counties. By 2007, the population had increased such that 69.4 percent of Cubans living in the United States resided in Florida, with only 5.2 percent in California and 5.5 percent in New Jersey. Moreover, of those Cubans who immigrated after the Mariel boatlift (i.e., those who immigrated since 1980), 80.5 percent reside in Florida, with only 3.3 percent residing in New Jersey, 3 percent in California, and less than 2 percent residing in New York.

Paralleling the changes immediately following the Cuban revolution, the magnitude of the influx of post-Mariel immigrants has been striking. In 2000, pre- and post-Mariel immigrants constituted about equal portions of the Cuban American population (37.6 percent vs. 37.4 percent) in the state of Florida while the native born accounted for the remainder. By 2007, these trends were reflected nationally as post-Mariel immigrants constituted a majority (52.8 percent) of foreign-born Cuban Americans and 32.4 percent of the Cuban American community while pre-Mariel immigrants constituted 31.3 percent.

The Mariel Boatlift

In the spring of 1980, following the Cuban government's siege of the Peruvian embassy in Havana with thousands of asylum-seeking Cubans inside, Fidel Castro temporarily allowed all those who wanted to leave Cuba to do so. This policy fostered the boatlift from the port of Mariel, which occurred from late April through September of 1980. As these émigrés had to find their own way out of Cuba, and owing to South Florida's proximity, it became the logical destination for many of these refugees. About 125,000 Cubans immigrated to the United States during this period.

Mariel is significant not just for the large number of people who left Cuba, but perhaps most importantly because it signaled the arrival of a new type of émigré. In general, those who left prior to Mariel were political refugees who flourished in Batista's Cuba but struggled with the revolution. These immigrants tended to hold higher skilled jobs and were more likely to have had property seized and relatives persecuted, imprisoned, or tortured at the hands of the Castro government. In addition, upon arriving in the United States, these immigrants were able to avail themselves of a variety of "Great Society" programs that would help foster their economic success.

Today, these pre-Mariel refugees are devoutly Republican, a phenomenon that stems from two primary sources. First, this group's support for the GOP emanates from the party's strong anti-Communist stand as well as their perception that the Democratic Party has repeatedly bungled U.S. Cuba policy. The disastrous Bay of Pigs invasion [under the John F. Kennedy administration], the inadequate response to the shoot-down of humanitarian rescue planes by Cuban Migs in 1996 [under Democrat Bill Clinton], and the repatriation of Elián González in 2000 are just a few examples of how, on the issues important to Cuban Americans, Democrats have repeatedly opposed them. Reinforcing this Republican affiliation, Cuban Americans' economic success has made them receptive to Republicans' pro-business and small government platforms.

Post-Mariel immigrants, in contrast, were socialized in revolutionary Cuba and tend to have had little experience with Batista's Cuba. Unlike the pre-Mariel immigrants, their motivation to emigrate was less political and more directly tied to the desire for increased economic opportunity. They were less likely to be economically well off while living in Cuba and are more likely to have close ties to people who remain on the island. Moreover, given their very different life experiences, post-Mariel immigrants living in the United States earn about 50 percent less ($14,194 vs. $22,638) and are less likely to have a college degree (18.8% vs. 26.9%) than are the pre-Mariel immigrants.

The surge of post-Mariel Cubans into the United States and especially Florida is potentially quite important because to the extent that we see a shift in attitudes in the Cuban American community, they may be driven by these groups' very different life experiences, socioeconomic circumstances, and opportunities both in Cuba prior to their leaving and in the United States once they arrived. . . .

Why Won't Little Havana Turn Blue?

The remarkable change in the demographic composition and attitudes of the Cuban American community over the past twenty years leads one to question why we don't see more support for Democratic candidates among Cuban American voters. While one might be inclined to view the 2008 presidential election as a new benchmark for Democrats as John McCain "only" won 63.9 percent of the Cuban American vote, this total is still large relative to the 60.5 percent garnered by Bob Dole in 1996. Moreover, in each of the three 2008 South Florida congressional races in which Cuban American Republican incumbents (i.e., Ileana Ros-Lehtinen, Mario Diaz-Balart, and Lincoln Diaz-Balart) were challenged by Cuban American Democrats, the Republican won handily. In the races for the seats held by Mario and Lincoln Diaz-Balart, the Republican candidates won despite the Democratic Party recruiting strong challengers and providing substantial financial support.

Predictions of change stem from the observation that the changing demographics will alter the political makeup of the Cuban American community; however, several factors seem to portend moderation in Cuban Americans' voting behavior. First, members of the second and third generations are increasingly entering the community and electorate. Conventional wisdom suggests that having not experienced Communist Cuba, these native-born voters may not feel the passion for the issues that relate to it. As one person we spoke with noted, "To my kids Castro is just a guy dad tells stories about." Moreover, as we saw in the previous section, once resource differences are considered, we observe significant generational differences in attitudes and partisanship. Second, because of the influx of new immigrants and the passing of the older exiles, demographic trends depict a community that increasingly consists of post-Mariel immigrants. As with the generational effects, these cohort differences are also manifest in attitudes and partisan differences. . . .

While these differences in date of immigration go some distance in helping to explain the disjunctive between policy attitudes, partisanship, and the vote, by themselves they do little to explain why Little Havana refuses to turn blue. . . .

One explanation for this puzzle might stem from differences in the composition of the Cuban American community versus the Cuban American voting electorate. More specifically, if post-Mariel immigrants were underrepresented at the ballot box, then we might expect to see higher levels of support for McCain among voters than among the community as a whole.

An examination of the proportion of Cuban American voters in South Florida who immigrated before and after 1980 suggests that there is likely some merit to this argument. Despite post-Mariel immigrants constituting a majority of foreign-born Cubans in the community, in both 2004 and 2008, 78.6 percent and 71.7 percent of the Cuban American *electorate* consisted of pre-Mariel immigrants. Moreover, while the increase in participation among post-Mariel immigrants between 2004 and 2008 (from 21.6 percent to 28.3 percent) is far too small to explain the entire gap, it is also consistent with the decreased support for John McCain compared to George Bush as the proportion of post-Mariel immigrants that voted increased by about 6 percent between 2004 and 2008.

Incorporation and Immigration

What explains the fact that the Cuban American electorate continues to be dominated by pre-Mariel immigrants? Research on political incorporation frequently emphasizes the role that formal (i.e., government policies) and informal (e.g., competitive elections) institutions play in facilitating immigrant political incorporation. Others studying the incorporation of Cubans find that the institutional contexts from which the migrants left and to which they arrived both affect the ease of incorporation in society. Perhaps the most plausible explanations for this stunning gap in voter turnout between pre- and post-Mariel immigrants can be attributed to institutional and socioeconomic factors that may disproportionately inhibit post-Mariel immigrants.

Institutionally, the unique immigration policy that allows Cuban immigrants who make it to U.S. soil to stay and work is scarcely different than that faced by pre-Mariel immigrants under the Cuban Adjustment Act of 1966. This policy holds that once in the United States, Cubans need not rush to obtain citizenship as virtually all Cubans are eligible for permanent residency after residing in the United States for one year. Owing to these conditions, attitude differences between pre- and post-Mariel Cuban immigrants are more likely to be rooted in other institutional and socioeconomic circumstances.

The U.S. government's receptivity toward new immigrants has decreased since the 1960s, and especially since the election of Ronald Reagan in 1980. Owing to the less generous welfare state policies, post-Mariel immigrants face a less welcoming social context in which the state takes a much more laissez-faire role in assisting immigrant assimilation when contrasted with the experience of earlier Cuban immigrants. The less welcoming context, combined with the lower socioeconomic background of post-Mariel immigrants, may serve to increase the costs of political participation by implicitly limiting who can receive the right to vote by becoming a citizen. As the process of obtaining citizenship can be very expensive, the financial incentives are such that post-Mariel immigrants are effectively discouraged from voting, in contrast to the earliest Cuban refugees who, despite facing similar institutional hurdles, tended to enter the United States with greater resources and at a point in history that was more accommodating of their circumstances. Moreover, even those post-Mariel immigrants who want to bear the costs of becoming citizens must endure the torpid citizenship process, which under the 1966 Cuban Adjustment Act takes about five years. Immigrants who have not been in the United States this long are ineligible for citizenship and thus unable to vote.

To what extent do these institutional factors impede the participation of more recent immigrants? To answer this question, we use American Community Survey data from 2007 to compare the proportion of each of these immigrant groups that are qualified to vote (i.e., they are eighteen years old and citizens) from the pool of those who are theoretically eligible for citizenship by having been in the United States at least five years. The results show a dramatic gap: While about 90 percent of those who immigrated before Mariel are qualified, less than 46 percent of those who immigrated after 1980 are similarly qualified.

Similarly, we can also look to see if the participation rate among those who are qualified to vote (i.e., those who are over age eighteen and are citizens) is higher for those who immigrated before 1980 than for those who immigrated after. While the data on Cuban American immigrants from the 2008 American Community Survey November voting supplement are limited, the results are consistent with expectations. Of those who immigrated before 1980, 80.5 percent reported having voted, as compared to the 62.1 percent of the post-1980 immigrants who reported having done so.

Even absent the interactions with the institutions we describe earlier, socioeconomic factors by themselves seem likely to play a role as well since post-Mariel immigrants have lower socioeconomic status than do earlier Cuban immigrants. As socioeconomic status is strongly associated with the ability to pay the costs of voting, we would expect them to vote at lower rates, even if obtaining citizenship were costless and immediate. Finally, [Susan] Eckstein points out that these more recent immigrants were less likely to have been politically active in Cuba, and since political activity is habit forming, they are less likely to participate once in the United States.

Change Will Come, but Slowly

An often repeated joke in Miami holds that Democrats' best bet for making inroads in the Cuban American community lies in sending immigration lawyers to South Florida to help post-Mariel immigrants obtain citizenship. Our results suggest that while there may be some truth to this logic, the factors affecting Cuban Americans' attitudes and behavior are far more complex than such folk wisdom suggests. Examining the political implications for the changing demographics of the Cuban American community, we find substantial evidence that attitudes of Cuban Americans have undergone significant change driven largely by the introduction of post-Mariel immigrants, who hold more progressive attitudes, into the community. . . .

To the extent that all of these factors portend at least slightly more progressive political preferences, and consistent with past research on political incorporation, these trends suggest that Cuban American voters' strict allegiance to the GOP and strident support of bans on trade and travel will likely fade only gradually with time. It is important to note, however, that the process is occurring more slowly than pundits suggest. Staunch anti-Castro Republicans are not being replaced by either post-Mariel immigrants or later generations that are strong Democrats. Moreover, to the extent that their allegiances fade, presumably new political ties will develop based on issues that are not especially salient today. Candidates' battles over these issues will likely determine how Cuban Americans vote in the future.

Periodical and Internet Sources Bibliography

The following articles have been selected to supplement the diverse views presented in this chapter.

Lawrence Davidson	"Privatizing National Interest—The Cuba Lobby," *Kentucky Scholarship Online*, September 2011. http://kentucky.universitypressscholarship.com.
Jeffrey Goldberg	"It's Time to Remove Cuba from the State-Sponsor-of-Terrorism List," *Atlantic*, January 17, 2012.
Zaid Jilani	"It's Not Just Ozzie Guillen: How the Cuba Lobby Paralyzes U.S. Policy," *Republic Report*, April 10, 2012. www.republicreport.org.
Guillermo I. Martinez	"Why Cuban Americans Defy Predicted Changes in Voting Patterns," *Sun Sentinel* (Fort Lauderdale, FL), November 24, 2011.
Bettye Miller	"Cuban American Voters Remain in GOP Corner," UCR Today, January 30, 2012. http://ucrtoday.ucr.
Alejandro Guevara Onofre	"The Pro-Castro Lobby in Latin America," Yahoo! Voices, February 13, 2011. http://voices.yahoo.com.
Nicky Pear	"Seeds of Change Emerge in the Havana/Miami/Washington Triangle," *The Cutting Edge*, November 1, 2010. www.thecuttingedgenews.com.
Geoff Thale	"Republican Candidates Compete for the Shrinking Voting Bloc of Hardline Cuban Americans," Washington Office on Latin America, January 31, 2012. www.wola.org.

OPPOSING
VIEWPOINTS®
SERIES

CHAPTER 4

What Should Be the US Policy Toward Cuba?

Chapter Preface

The United States–Cuba relationship has long been antagonistic. Indeed, the relationship has been so bad that for years the United States actively attempted to assassinate Cuba's authoritarian leader, Fidel Castro.

US assassination attempts were, of course, secret. However, according to Dan Bohning in a February 19, 2008, essay on CNN, many details of the plots were revealed during a 1975 Senate investigation. More details were revealed in 1993, Bohning explained, when a report on the assassination plots was declassified.

Bohning said that there were at least eight plots to assassinate Castro between 1960 and 1965, only some of which were actually put into effect. However, Duncan Campbell writing in an August 2, 2006, article in the *Guardian* suggested there may have been many more. Fabian Escalante, who was one of Castro's guards, said that there were more than six hundred plots, though how many of these were orchestrated by the United States is unclear.

One of the more outlandish plots involved Castro's well-known fondness for scuba diving. American intelligence proposed planting a large, eye-catching seashell near Castro's usual scuba-diving route; when Castro went to investigate, the shell would explode. The plot was abandoned, however, because there was no good way to place the shell. In another plot, a former lover was paid to kill Castro with poisoned cold cream; she reportedly backed out at the last minute.

Other plots against Castro were simpler—some involved nothing more than hiring gangsters to shoot him. Campbell reported that there was even an attempt against Castro's life as recently as 2000, though US intelligence involvement has not been proven. The plot involved explosives planted under a podium at which Castro was to speak in Panama. The attempt was carried out by four members of the Cuban-exile community, including former Central Intelligence Agency (CIA) operative Luis Posada. Posada denied involvement in the plot and was released from jail following a controversial pardon by Panamanian president Mireya Moscoso in 2004.

In the face of so many death threats, Castro and his security team became very cautious. In the early period after the revolution, he would sometimes go out alone into the streets, but such activities were curtailed. For much of his long reign, he used doubles and moved between twenty different addresses to foil attackers, according to Campbell.

Castro has been ill since 2006, and he stepped down from the presidency in favor of his brother, Raúl. The assassination attempts on Fidel contributed to the long-term tensions between the United States and Cuba. They also were good propaganda for Castro, who could claim with some justice that the United States was illegally and violently interfering in Cuban affairs. Ironically, US and Cuban émigré efforts to kill Castro may have been part of what helped the dictator cling to power for so long.

Given such a tense relationship, there are many controversies involving US policy toward Cuba. The authors of the viewpoints in the following chapter examine several of them, including whether the United States should improve relations with Cuba, whether it should continue the trade embargo, and whether it should return Guantánamo Bay to Cuba.

"Travel to Cuba enriches, entrenches and thus emboldens the regime to shrug off criticism and sharpen its fangs."

The United States Must Maintain the Embargo Against Cuba

Humberto Fontova

Humberto Fontova is a conservative Cuban American blogger and political commentator, as well as the author of Fidel: Hollywood's Favorite Tyrant. *In the following viewpoint, he argues that the Cuban embargo by America is ineffectual and that tourism to Cuba is at all-time highs. He adds that Cuban repression has only increased as tourism has increased. He further argues that advocates of dismantling the embargo are in the pay of Cuban business interests. He concludes that the embargo should be tightened and that tourism to Cuba aids the repressive Castro regime.*

As you read, consider the following questions:

1. Why does Fontova say it makes sense to allow Americans to travel to Cuba but not to North Korea?

2. What funds from America to Cuba make it laughable to label Cuba policy an embargo, according to Fontova?

3. Who is Phil Peters, and why does Fontova believe he is not objective on Cuba policy?

"More travel to Cuba means more freedom for Cubans," goes the anti-"embargo" mantra.

Tourism and Repression

Now here's what a recent story by Reuters out of Havana said: "Cuba just completed its best year for tourism with 2.7 million visitors in 2011. Hotels are full to the brim and Old Havana, the capital's historic center, is teeming with tourists from around the world.... 'We are at capacity ... totally full,' said the manager of a foreign hotel company."

Now here's a recent report by the Cuban Commission for Human Rights [and National Reconciliation] as reported by Martí Noticias: "December 2011 was the worst month for political arrests in 30 years. Elizardo Sánchez said 'all signs are indicating that ... the regime *has greatly ramped up its repressive machinery*.' ... This indicates that the regime has *granted top priority to the institutions of repression*."

In the 1950s when Cuba hosted an average 200,000 tourists annually, it was billed as a "tourist playground." Well, for *two* decades now Cuba has been hosting from *five to ten times* the number of tourists annually as it hosted in the 1950s. Result?

The Heritage Foundation's Index of Economic Freedom shows no loosening in Cuba's repression during this tourism windfall. For over a decade Cuba has consistently ranked as the most economically repressive regime in the hemisphere and among the four most repressive on earth, consistently nudging North Korea for top honors.

"But if Americans can legally travel to North Korea," comes the reflexive retort, "why not to Cuba?"

Because tourism represents a tiny source of income for North Korea's terror-sponsoring regime, whereas it represents the main life support (right behind Venezuelan subsidies) of Cuba's terror-sponsoring regime. So the United States applies a different type of sanctions to Stalinist North Korea than to Stalinist Cuba.

As shown earlier, the evidence, proof and verdict on Cuba travel are all in. Rather than soothing the savage beast of Castroism [that is, the regime of Cuban dictator Fidel Castro], travel to Cuba enriches, entrenches and thus emboldens the regime to shrug off criticism and sharpen its fangs.

But point this out and "experts" on the matter will unanimously denounce you as "embittered," "irrational" and "blinded by emotion."

For much of the past decade, the United States has been among Cuba's biggest food suppliers. The expenditures by an estimated 400,000 travelers from the United States combined with a blizzard of remittances [money from Cuban families abroad] puts the estimated cash flow from the United States to Cuba last year [2011] at $4 billion. While a proud Soviet satrapy, Cuba received $3 billion to $5 billion annually from the Soviets. So to label our current relationship with Cuba an "embargo" is laughable.

To label it a "blockade" shows appalling ignorance, functional illiteracy—or more likely—Castro-regime advocacy, on its payroll or off. And given the absence of any person or entity registered with U.S. Department of Justice as agents of the Cuban government, we have to assume the latter.

Castro's Payroll

Payments from Castro's payroll, however, can appear in laundered form. Take the case of the oft-quoted (especially here at the *Miami Herald*) champion of unfettered U.S. travel to Cuba, Phil Peters of the Lexington Institute. A LexisNexis search

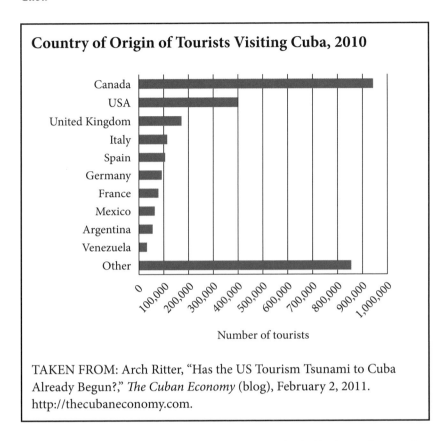

Country of Origin of Tourists Visiting Cuba, 2010

Number of tourists

TAKEN FROM: Arch Ritter, "Has the US Tourism Tsunami to Cuba Already Begun?," *The Cuban Economy* (blog), February 2, 2011. http://thecubaneconomy.com.

shows that Mr. Peters could be properly billed as the mainstream media's "go-to" source on the Cuba "embargo" issue.

Well, here's some background on the Lexington Institute's funding:

In a joint venture with the Castro regime, Canadian mining company Sherritt International operates the Moa nickel mining plant in Cuba's Oriente province. This facility was stolen by Castro gunmen from its U.S. managers and stockholders at Soviet gunpoint in 1960 (when it was worth $90 million.) Now here's something from a legal memo uncovered by *Babalú Blog* as part of a court case discovery: "Canada's Sherritt works quietly in Washington . . . *recently it has given money to a former State Department employee, Phil Peters, to advance its interests.* The money to Peters goes through contributions to the Lexington Institute, where Peters is a vice president. Because the Lexington Institute is a 501(c) (3) not-for-profit, there is no public record of Sherritt's funding. This has allowed Peters to advise and direct the [House of Representatives] Cuba Working Group (a congressional anti-embargo cabal) in ways beneficial to Sherritt *while presenting himself to the group as an objective think tank scholar."*

In brief: One of the Castro regime's top business partners funnels under-the-table payments to America's top anti-embargo publicist, who is invariably billed as an "impartial scholarly expert" in every media mention.

And in brief: Every shred of observable evidence proves that travel to Cuba enriches and entrenches the KGB-trained [that is, trained by Soviet Russia's intelligence service] and heavily armed owners of Cuba's tourism industry, and thus the most highly motivated guardians of Cuba's Stalinist status quo.

> *"The United Nations General Assembly (UNGA) on Oct. 25 adopted a resolution on the need to end the economic, commercial and financial embargo imposed by the US against Cuba."*

VN Supports UN Call for End of Embargo Against Cuba

Vietnamese News Agency

On its website, the Vietnamese News Agency (VNA) offers constantly updated news on domestic and international socioeconomic affairs, culture, science, and technology. In the following viewpoint, the author reports the firm support of Vietnam and other United Nations (UN) member states for the resolution on the need to end the US embargo against Cuba. After reporting on US violation of international law and the Cubans' economic hardship resulting from the embargo, the author notes that 2011 was the twentieth year that the UN resolution had been adopted.

As you read, consider the following questions:

1. Who is Le Hoang Trung, according to the viewpoint?

2. What six groups or regions within the United Nations joined together in supporting the resolution to end the embargo?

Vietnamese News Agency, "VN Supports UN Call for End of Embargo Against Cuba," October 26, 2011. Reproduced by permission.

3. Who is Vitaly Churkin, and what was his opinion on the embargo?

October 26, 2011 (VNA)—The United Nations General Assembly (UNGA) on Oct. 25 adopted a resolution on the need to end the economic, commercial and financial embargo imposed by the US against Cuba with 186 ayes, two noes and three blank votes. At the UNGA plenary session, permanent representative of Vietnam Ambassador Le Hoang Trung said, "Vietnam shares the view of the international community that the US should end the embargo against Cuba". The policies and measures in pursuit of the embargo against Cuba, including the "Helms-Burton Act", go against international law and the purposes and principles of the United Nations Charter, hinder the development of friendly relations among nations, and violate the right of people to self-determination, to determine their political system and path of development, said the Vietnamese diplomat. The restrictions in trade, finance and even travel continue to have serious illegal extraterritorial effects on the sovereignty of other states as well as efforts towards an equal and just global economic structure for the prosperity of every nation, said Trung. Representatives of members of G-77 [Group of 77 at the United Nations] group, the Non-Aligned Movement, the African Union, the Caribbean Community, MERCOSUR (the Common Market of the South) and the Organisation of Islamic Cooperation strongly condemned the US embargo, affirming that it has violated the international law and gone against the UN Charter. They demanded that the US implement the UNGA's resolutions and immediately put an end to its illegal embargo against Cuba. Cuban Foreign Minister [FM] Bruno Rodriguez Parrilla valued the international community's support to Havana's legitimate struggle to demand Washington to lift its irrational embargo unconditionally. The US policy on Cuba has seriously violated international law and human rights, said the Cuban FM. Meanwhile,

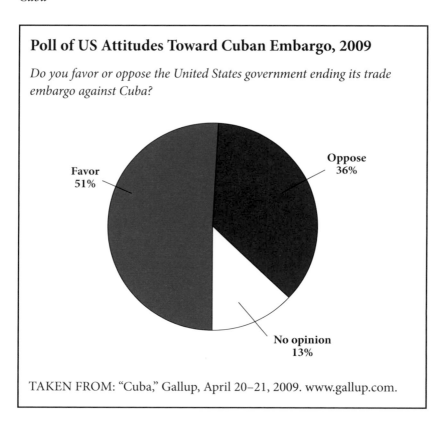

Poll of US Attitudes Toward Cuban Embargo, 2009

Do you favor or oppose the United States government ending its trade embargo against Cuba?

Favor
51%

Oppose
36%

No opinion
13%

TAKEN FROM: "Cuba," Gallup, April 20–21, 2009. www.gallup.com.

Russian ambassador to the UN Vitaly Churkin affirmed that discrimination measures, including the embargo, are totally unacceptable in the current context and they are evidence of a rude intervention into Cuba's internal affairs. This is the 20th consecutive year the UNGA adopted a resolution on the issue.

"Domestic politics dictates international policy, even when it leads to actions that are plainly unproductive."

US Policy Toward Cuba Is Rooted in Domestic Politics

Ronald Sanders

Ronald Sanders is a former senior Caribbean ambassador. In the following viewpoint, he argues that Barack Obama's decision to exclude Cuba from the Summit of the Americas was driven by domestic politics. Specifically, he says that Obama wants to win the state of Florida in 2012 and that his Cuba policy is a way to pander to the anti-Castro Cuban community in that state. Sanders says that placing domestic concerns first is understandable. However, he concludes that the result of the United States' domestic driven isolation of Cuba is counterproductive and actually helps entrench the authoritarian Cuban regime.

As you read, consider the following questions:

1. Why does Sanders say that Canada supported Cuba's exclusion from the Summit of the Americas?

2. Why does Sanders say that most Latin American nations support Cuba's *inclusion* in the Summit of the Americas?

3. According to Sanders, why does Cuba's government dismiss the Organization of American States?

US President Barack Obama vetoed Cuba's attendance at this month's [April 2012's] Summit of the Americas in Colombia for domestic political reasons. He was not alone in applying domestic considerations. Every other hemispheric leader adopted a position on Cuba that related to his/her own political concerns.

Domestic Issues Drive Hemispheric Politics

Canada's prime minister, Stephen Harper, supported Obama in denying an invitation not only to the Colombia summit but also to the next one in Panama in 2015 because he had an eye on the importance of maintaining a close link to the US. The US is Canada's biggest trading partner, and to preserve that position, it is as well that the Canadian government be seen by all parties in the US as supportive of US policies.

Of course, unlike other countries in the Western Hemisphere, including all who now call for Cuba's participation in the Summit of the Americas, Canada has always maintained diplomatic relations with Cuba and trade has continued briskly between the two nations. Therefore, notwithstanding Fidel Castro's lambasting of Stephen Harper after he criticised Cuba's human rights record, there is more than enough economic benefits for Cuba in its relations with Canada for the Castro government not to allow this event to mar the overall association between the two countries.

As for the Caribbean countries, almost all of them now benefit from Cuba's scholarship programme for their young people to study at Cuban universities, as well as Cuba's programme of supplying doctors and other forms of technical assistance. They know that the Cuban government provides this assistance at great cost to itself. The resources could be used to address serious problems within Cuba, not least shortages of food and medicines. They also know that Cuba is now no military threat to the United States and has no interest in military adventurism anywhere in the hemisphere.

Further, despite the fact that Cuba still remains on the US State Department's list of "state sponsors of terrorism". Caribbean governments also know that this listing is without foundation and should be abandoned.

In calling for Cuba's inclusion in meetings of the Summit of the Americas—in the face of opposition from the US government—Caribbean governments are paying back Cuba for its generous assistance to them.

Human Rights Are a Concern

Of course, Barack Obama is correct when he makes the following observation about Caribbean governments and the relatively new "democratic" governments in Latin America: "I am sometimes puzzled by the degree to which countries that themselves have undergone enormous transformations, that have known the oppression of dictatorships or have found themselves on the wrong side of the ruling elite, and have suffered for it, why we would ignore that same principle here."

It is obvious that Obama, the man, is concerned that "Cuba has not yet moved to democracy, has not yet observed basic human rights." It is the same concern that Stephen Harper identified. There is validity in the unease, and the Cuban government must do more—and do it more openly—to end its regime of intolerance to dissent and its resistance to political change. Other countries in the hemisphere, including all the nations of the Caribbean, have learned to accommodate political dissent, to respond to demands of workers, to hold elections, and to change governments by peaceful means.

The question that always arises on this issue is whether Cuba should be encouraged to undergo the required change

Obama and Cuba

In 2009, President [Barack] Obama made his first mark on the presidency in relation to Cuba by easing travel restrictions to Cuba, but only for Cuban Americans. . . . The [George W.] Bush administration had restricted travel for Cuban Americans to the island, resulting in three-year delays between visits and limitations on supplies and money that could be sent to the island. In contrast, President Obama eliminated travel restrictions for all Cuban Americans and restored the amount of remittances families could send to the island to their original levels. His administration has also eased visa restrictions for artists to travel to the island, creating opportunity for cultural and academic exchanges that can hopefully segue into greater dialogue between both nations.

The Cuban government has applauded this policy shift, and in terms of normalizing of relations with the island, it is certainly a step in the right direction. It should also be noted that this action was well received by the Cuban American community, with nearly 250,000 Cuban Americans visiting the island during 2009. Despite the anti-Castro rhetoric, close to half of all Cuban Americans have returned to their homeland for visits and have no problem spending American dollars in Cuba.

Matthew B. Stieglitz, "Constructive Engagement: The Need
for a Progressive Cuban Lobby in Obama's Washington,"
Center for the Study of the Presidency & Congress, 2010–2011.
www.thepresidency.org.

by isolation or by engagement. The US has chosen isolation through the trade embargo and resisting Cuba's attendance at the Americas Summit. The matter of membership of the Organization of American States (OAS) is no longer relevant since the Castro government has described the organisation as "an unburied corpse". But, that is more bluster on the Cuban government's part than an accurate assessment of the OAS. The organisation is now more concerned with democratic governance in its member states than it used to be, and the Cuban government would find it difficult to measure up to the criteria for securing and maintaining membership.

Neither Obama nor Harper has sought to defend their denial of Cuba's participation in the Americas Summit while they engage with China in several fora despite the latter's human rights record. Yet, if they argue that engagement with China is essential to promoting change, it should be equally necessary in Cuba's case. Hence, they should drop their objection to Cuba's participation in the summit and use it as a forum for setting and applying principles to which all countries, including Cuba, would have to adhere.

The Politics of Florida

But, Obama, the president of the US who is seeking another term in office, has to deal with carrying the state of Florida in the upcoming presidential election. Florida, where many influential anti-Castro, Cuban Americans live, is important to winning the presidency. Given the strong anti-Castro feeling, Obama could not afford to offend the Florida electorate by agreeing to the Cuban government's participation at the Colombia summit, nor could he signal now that he would agree to its attendance in Panama in 2015. Like every other leader, domestic politics dictates international policy, even when it leads to actions that are plainly unproductive.

A clear indication that anti-Castro sentiment is very much alive and well in Florida is the passage by the legislature last March of a bill designed to punish the Castro government by restricting state and local governments from signing procurement contracts with any companies that do business with Cuba. The constitutionality of such a bill has been questioned since "only the federal government (and Congress) has the legislative competence to conduct foreign policy and impose sanctions". But, it would be a foolishly daring Obama who would veto the bill.

Domestic politics in the US trumps a more sensible policy of engagement with Cuba. The crazy thing is that it suits the Castro regime since they can continue to blame the "Yankee imperialists" for the deprived conditions the Cuban people suffer. For the Cuban leadership, as for all other hemispheric leaders, the imperatives of domestic politics triumph.

| "*During my trip, it hit me how much Guantánamo . . . is really a part of Cuba.*"

The United States Should Give Guantánamo Bay Back to Cuba

Julia E. Sweig

Julia E. Sweig is a senior fellow at the Council on Foreign Relations and the author of Cuba: What Everyone Needs to Know. *In the following viewpoint, she argues that the United States should return the military base at Guantánamo, Cuba, to Cuban control. She argues that the base has already been a venue for Cuban American cooperation. In addition, because of accusations of US torture and human rights abuses, the base has become an international political liability. She argues that giving up the base could break the stalemate in US-Cuban relations and reduce tensions between the two countries.*

As you read, consider the following questions:

1. What does Sweig say is Guantánamo's minor strategic value to the United States?

2. What is the annual rent of Guantánamo, and what does Cuba do with the money, according to Sweig?

3. What does Sweig say should be a first step toward using Guantánamo to reduce tensions with Cuba?

President [Barack] Obama has promised to shut down the detention camp at Guantánamo Bay, seeking to erase a blot on America's global image.[1] He has also reached out to Cuba, easing some travel and financial restrictions in an effort to recast Washington's approach to the island. These two initiatives have proceeded on separate tracks so far, but now is the time to bring them together. Hiding in plain sight, the U.S. naval base at Guantánamo Bay is the ideal place for Obama to launch a far-reaching transformation of Washington's relationship with its Communist neighbor.

How? By preparing to give Guantánamo back to Cuba.

End the Stalemate

It's not as impossible as it sounds. The United States has scaled back, modified or even withdrawn its military presence elsewhere; think Okinawa, South Korea, Subic Bay in the Philippines or Vieques in Puerto Rico. Whatever Guantánamo's minor strategic value to the United States for processing refugees or as a counter-narcotics outpost, the costs of staying permanently—with the stain of the prisons, the base's imperial legacy and the animosity of the host government—outweigh the benefits.

The time to begin this transition is now. By transforming Guantánamo as part of a broader remaking of Washington's relationship with Cuba, the Obama administration can begin fixing what the president himself has decried as a "failed" policy. It can upend a U.S.-Cuba stalemate that has barely

---

1. Guantánamo Bay has been used since September 11, 2001, to detain those accused of terrorism. The United States has been accused of ignoring the rights of, and torturing, prisoners held there.

budged for 50 years and can put to the test [Cuban president] Raúl Castro's stated willingness to entertain meaningful changes.

A Part of Cuba

I visited the 45-square-mile U.S. naval base at the southeastern tip of Cuba last month [April 2009] at the invitation of Adm. James Stavridis, head of U.S. Southern Command. I went less to see the prison cells or learn about detainee treatment (though I did both) than to explore a region that I'd never visited in a quarter century of traveling to and writing about the island. I not only wanted to see what was actually happening there, but also to imagine how the base could evolve once the detention facility is shut down and the eyes of the world shift elsewhere.

During my trip, it hit me how much Guantánamo—two-thirds of which is made up of the pristine waters of the bay that bears the same name—is really a part of Cuba. Overlooking the western side of the bay sat a pair of well-kept 1940s-style houses, precise replicas of the kind of residences I had seen in Havana weeks earlier. I hadn't expected the natural environment to capture my attention the way it did. Manatees, which are disappearing elsewhere, breed in abundance; dolphins dart out of mangrove swamps and swim alongside the Navy's ferries and motor crafts as they cross the bay.

Driving along the fence line and seeing the Cuban flags and watchtowers, I was struck by the relative peace and quiet that both sides maintain at the one spot where they deal with each other most. In a way, when flag officers and staff from both sides meet each month at the base's east gate, they continue a long history of pragmatic if ambivalent engagement that started well before Guantánamo became the nightmarish Gitmo [a nickname for the detention center].

After the United States intervened in the Spanish-American War in 1898, Washington forced Cuba to accept the creation of a naval coaling station at Guantánamo Bay in 1903 as a condition of independence. During several peak years of activity and construction in the 1940s, at least 9,000 Cuban civilians worked on the base, and small cities such as Caimanera and Boquerón catered to foreign soldiers with bars, brothels and the like. During the revolution, Cubans smuggled all sorts of supplies off the base to aid the rebel cause. Even after 1959, as the new Castro regime sharpened its attacks on symbols of American power, working on the base did not necessarily preclude being a good revolutionary. To this day, the United States provides pension benefits and health care to a handful of retired Cuban workers, some of whom still live on the base.

Since the Bay of Pigs invasion [in 1961, when a Central Intelligence Agency–trained force of Cuban exiles tried unsuccessfully to invade Cuba and overthrow the government] more than four decades ago, Havana has demanded the return of the base territory, but Washington has found little incentive to leave. The base is a financial freebie; the annual rent is only $4,000, although on grounds of pride and principle, Cuba has not cashed the check since 1959.

Yet the Cuban government has never taken steps, military or otherwise, to get the base back. "We are audacious and valiant," remarked Cuban president Osvaldo Dorticós in 1964, "but we are not stupid." Echoing such practicality, Raúl Castro has referred to Guantánamo as a "neutral place" where dialogue with the Obama administration might one day unfold.

Since the 1990s, the monthly "fence-line" talks have ensured safety for the people who work in and around Guantánamo's air, land and maritime borders. Shortly after the United States began housing terrorism suspects at the base, Raúl Castro even offered to send back any detainee who tried to escape into Cuban territory. But as allegations of torture emerged and Guantánamo's symbolism went global, Cuba joined the world in excoriating the United States.

Despite the glimmers of political will on both sides, a rapprochement between Washington and Havana will take time. Obama has called for the release of Cuba's political prisoners. Cuba has its eye on the dismantling of American commercial sanctions and the return of Cuban spies now serving lengthy sentences in U.S. jails. The Castro brothers are unlikely to frame any reforms as a concession to Washington, while the Obama administration will wait to see how the government of Raúl Castro fulfills its commitment to "improve the material and spiritual lives of the Cuban people."

Ideology-Free Zone

Of course, just as Obama is not going to lift the embargo tomorrow, neither will he simply give back the base the next day. But short of anything so bold, the two governments and their armed forces have already shown that Guantánamo can eventually become an ideology-free zone.

The two nations could expand their monthly gate talks beyond the issue of perimeter security to include drug trafficking, human smuggling, refugee processing and disaster preparedness and relief. Such confidence-building talks could lead to deeper cooperation, even on human rights and political prisoners.

Next, the United States should invite those same Cuban officers to cross the gates and tour Guantánamo, in part to view evidence of the Navy's stewardship of the natural environment—dimension of the American presence that is bound to challenge Cuban preconceptions. Third, hundreds of U.S. and international journalists, lawyers and refugee experts have visited the base in the past few years. Surely we can extend the same courtesy to their Cuban peers.

Finally, the Navy could invite public health professionals from Cuba, the United States and other countries in the region to the base to develop strategies for cooperation. Proposals to convert the base to a public health research and treat-

The Prison and the Base

One afternoon, I toured the fence line that separates the base [at Guantánamo Bay] from Cuba. My tour began at the northeast gate. . . . The official contact point between the base and Cuba, the northeast gate is where a dwindling number of Cuban "commuters," as Cuban laborers are called, enter the base each day for work. I was struck by the utter desolation of the place. No hostility. No people to sustain a grudge—in fact, no people at all. An old barracks that held up to 150 U.S. Marines at the time of the Cuban missile crisis [in 1962] is the solitary reminder of the gate's symbolic importance. . . .

In the several years before 9/11 [the September 11, 2001, terrorist attacks on the United States], the base functioned at "minimum pillar," navy parlance for maintaining just enough U.S. presence at the bay to prevent Castro from claiming that the base had been abandoned. From an outsider's perspective, minimum pillar persists. . . . The base's general state of disrepair became starker still in contrast to the new prison camp, where on my three visits to the bay everything appeared amply funded. We cruised by the so-called playground where "good prisoners" are allowed to take fresh air. "Fifteen million dollars," muttered my host. "That's the site of the new twenty-five-million-dollar permanent prison. . . . There, the twenty-million-dollar mental health clinic." Navy people console themselves that without the base you couldn't have the prison, but from a visitor's perspective it seems that the prison has all but become the base.

Jonathan M. Hansen, Guantánamo:
An American History. *New York: Hill and Wang, 2011.*

ment center date back to the [John F.] Kennedy White House and have been viewed favorably by Havana ever since, especially in light of Cuba's world-class expertise in infectious and tropical diseases.

These initiatives defy the argument that the United States should cling to the base—and the embargo, for that matter—as leverage to push Cuba toward democracy. The past 50 years have proven the fallacy of that logic. Returning Guantánamo Bay to full Cuban sovereignty and control is a win for the United States: Aside from the boon to America's credibility with the Cuban people and throughout Latin America, these first steps would probe the Cuban government's apparent disposition to use the base as a point of contact with the United States—and gauge the regime's willingness to move the ball forward even more.

"As a president, I say the U.S. should go. As a military man, I say let them stay," Raúl Castro quipped last year. It's hard to know exactly what he means. Floating these proposals would be a good way to find out.

| *"Cuba occupies an extraordinarily important geographic position for the United States."*

Beneath the US Obsession with Cuba

George Friedman

George Friedman is the founder and chief executive officer of Stratfor as well as the author of The Next 100 Years: A Forecast for the 21st Century. *In the following viewpoint, he argues that American interest in Cuba is ultimately based on geopolitical factors, not on domestic politics. He argues that Cuba is geographically positioned in such a way that it could be a base from which to interfere with US shipping and seriously damage US strategic interests. The United States, he says, has therefore been historically worried that a great power would dominate Cuba and present a threat to America. This fear, he says, has always been at the base of Cuba policy.*

As you read, consider the following questions:

1. Why does Friedman say that the US embargo has been more important for the Cuban regime than for the United States?

2. According to Friedman, how did the Guantánamo Bay naval base solve America's Cuban problem?

3. Why did Cuba become a minor issue for the United States after the end of the Cold War, according to Friedman?

The Cuban American National Foundation (CANF), a group vehemently opposed to the Cuban government, came out in favor of easing the U.S. isolation of Cuba last week. The move opens the possibility that the United States might shift its policies toward Cuba. Florida is a key state for anyone who wants to become president of the United States, and the Cuban community in Florida is substantial. Though the Soviet threat expired long ago, easing the embargo on Cuba has always held limited value to American politicians with ambitions. For them, Florida is more important than Cuba. Therefore, this historic shift alters the U.S. domestic political landscape.

In many ways, the U.S. policy of isolating Cuba has been more important to the Cubans than to the United States, particularly since the fall of the Soviet Union. The Cuban economy is in abysmal shape. But the U.S. embargo has been completely ineffective on the stated goal of destabilizing the Cuban government, which has used the embargo as justification for economic hardship. Although the embargo isolates Cuba from its natural market, the United States, the embargo is not honored by Canada, Mexico, Europe, China or anyone else beyond the United States. That means Cuban goods can be sold on the world market, Cuba can import anything it can pay for, and Cuba can get investment of any size from any country wishing to invest on the island. Because it has almost complete access to the global market, Cuba's economic problem is not the U.S. embargo. But the embargo does create a political defense for Cuban dysfunction.

It is easy to dismiss the embargo issue as primarily a matter of domestic politics for both nations. It is also possible to argue that, though Cuba was once significant to the United States, that significance has declined since the end of the Cold War. Both assertions are valid, but neither is sufficient. Beyond the apparently disproportionate U.S. obsession with Cuba, and beyond a Cuban government whose ideology pivots around anti-Americanism, there are deeper and more significant geopolitical factors to consider.

Cuba occupies an extraordinarily important geographic position for the United States. It sits astride the access points from the Gulf of Mexico into the Atlantic Ocean, and therefore is in a position to impact the export of U.S. agricultural products via the Mississippi River complex and New Orleans (not to mention the modern-day energy industrial centers along the Gulf Coast). If New Orleans is the key to the American Midwest's access to the world, Cuba is the key to New Orleans.

Access to the Atlantic from the Gulf runs on a line from Key West to the Yucatán Peninsula, a distance of about 380 miles. Running perpendicular through the middle of this line is Cuba. The Straits of Florida, the northern maritime passage from the Gulf to the Atlantic, is about 90 miles wide from Havana to Key West. The Yucatán Channel, the southern maritime passage, is about 120 miles wide. Cuba itself is about 600 miles long. On the northern route, the Bahamas run parallel to Cuba for about half that distance, forcing ships to the south, toward Cuba. On the southern route, after the Yucatán gantlet, the passage out of the Caribbean is made long and complicated by the West Indies. A substantial, hostile naval force or air power based in Cuba could blockade the Gulf of Mexico—and hence the American heartland.

Throughout the 19th century, Cuba was of concern to the United States for this reason. The moribund Spanish Empire controlled Cuba through most of the century, something the United States could live with. The real American fear was that the British—who had already tried for New Orleans itself in the War of 1812—would expel the Spanish from Cuba and take advantage of the island's location to strangle the United States. Lacking the power to do anything about Spain itself, the United States was content to rely on Madrid to protect Spanish interests and those of the United States.

Cuba remained a Spanish colony long after other Spanish colonies gained independence. The Cubans were intensely afraid of both the United States and Britain, and saw a relationship with Spain—however unpleasant—as more secure than risking English or American domination. The Cubans had mixed feelings about the prospect of formal independence from Spain followed by unofficial foreign domination.

But in 1895, the Cubans rose up against Spain (not for the first time) in what turned into the struggle that would culminate in the island's independence from the country. With a keen interest in Cuba, Washington declared war on Spain in 1898 and invaded Cuba. The Spanish were quickly defeated in the Spanish-American War and soon withdrew from the island. For the United States, the main goal was less about gaining control of Cuba itself (though that was the net result) than about denying Cuba to other world powers.

The United States solved its Cuban problem by establishing a naval base at Guantánamo Bay on the island. Between this base and U.S. naval bases in the Gulf and on the east coast, British naval forces in the Bahamas were placed in a vise. By establishing Guantánamo Bay on the southern coast of Cuba, near the Windward Passage between Cuba and Haiti, the United States controlled the southern route to the Atlantic through the Yucatán Channel.

For the United States, any power that threatened to establish a naval presence in Cuba represented a direct threat to U.S. national security. When there were fears during World War I that the Germans might seek to establish U-boat bases in Cuba—an unrealistic concern—the United States interfered

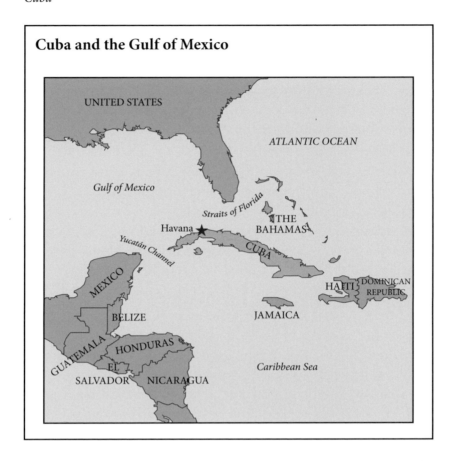

Cuba and the Gulf of Mexico

in Cuban politics to preclude that possibility. But it was the Soviet Union's presence in Cuba during the Cold War that really terrified the Americans.

From the Soviet point of view, Cuba served a purpose no other island in the region could serve. Missiles could be based in many places in the region, but only Cuba could bottle up the Gulf of Mexico. Any Soviet planner looking at a map would immediately identify Cuba as a key asset; any American planner looking at the same map would identify Cuba in Soviet hands as a key threat. For the Soviets, establishing a pro-Soviet regime in Cuba represented a geopolitical masterstroke. For the United States, it represented a geopolitical nightmare that had to be reversed.

Just as U.S. medium- and intermediate-range ballistic missiles in Turkey put the Soviet heartland in the crosshairs during the Cold War, Soviet missiles deployed operationally in Cuba put the entire U.S. eastern seaboard at risk. Mere minutes would have been available for detection and recognition of an attack before impact. In addition, the missiles' very presence would serve as a significant deterrent to conventional attack on the island—which is why it was so important for the United States not to allow an established missile presence in Cuba.

The final outcome of the U.S.-Soviet standoff pivoted on the Cuban missile crisis of 1962, which ended in an American blockade of Cuba, not a Soviet blockade of the Gulf. It was about missiles, not about maritime access. But the deal that ended the crisis solved the problem for the United States. In return for a U.S. promise not to invade Cuba, the Soviets promised not to place nuclear missiles on the island. If the Soviets didn't have missiles there, the United States could neutralize any naval presence in Cuba—and therefore any threat to American trade routes. Fidel Castro could be allowed to survive, but in a position of strategic vulnerability. One part of Washington's strategy was military, and the other part was economic—namely, the embargo.

Throughout Cuba's history as an independent nation, the Cubans simultaneously have viewed the United States as an economic driver of the Cuban economy, and as a threat to Cuban political autonomy. The Americans have looked at Cuba as a potential strategic threat. This imbalance made U.S. domination of Cuba inevitable. Cuban leaders in the first half of the 20th century accepted domination in return for prosperity. But there were those who argued that the island's prosperity was unequally distributed, and the loss of autonomy too damaging to accept. Castro led the latter group to success in the 1959 revolution against U.S.-supported Cuban president Fulgencio Batista. The anti-Castro émigrés who fled to the United States and established an influential community of anti-Castro sentiment had been part of the elite who prospered from Cuba's high level of dependence on the United States.

Cuban history has been characterized by an oscillation of views about the United States, with Cubans both wanting what it had to offer and seeking foreign powers—the Spanish, the British, the Soviets—to counterbalance the Americans. But the counterbalance either never materialized (in the case of the British) or, when it did, it was as suffocating as the Americans (in the case of the Soviets). In the end, Cuba probably would have preferred to be located somewhere not of strategic interest to the United States.

The U.S. obsession with Cuba does not manifest itself continuously; it appears only when a potentially hostile major power allies itself with Cuba and bases itself there. Cuba by itself can never pose a threat to the United States. Absent a foreign power, the United States is never indifferent to Cuba, but is much less sensitive. Therefore, after the end of the Cold War and the Soviet collapse, Cuba became a minor issue for the United States—and political considerations took precedence over geopolitical issues. Florida's electoral votes were more important than Cuba, and the status quo was left untouched.

Cuba has become a bit more important to the United States in the wake of the August 2008 Russo-Georgian war. In response to that conflict, the Americans sent warships into the Black Sea. The Russians responded by sending warships and strategic bombers into the Caribbean. High-profile Russian delegations have held talks with Cuba since then, increasing tensions. But these tensions are a tiny fraction of what they once were. Russia is in no way a strategic threat to American shipping in the Gulf of Mexico, nor is it going to be anytime soon, due to Russia's limited ability to wield substantive power in such a distant theater.

But Cuba is always an underlying concern to the United States. This concern can subside, but it cannot go away. Thus, from the American point of view, Russian probes are a reminder that Cuba remains a potential threat. Advocates of easing the embargo say it will help liberalize Cuba, just as trade relations liberalized Russia. The Cuban leadership shares this view and will therefore be very careful about how any liberalization is worked out. The Cubans must be thoroughly convinced of the benefits of increased engagement with the United States in order for Havana to sacrifice its ability to blame Washington for all of its economic problems. If Cuba opens too much to the United States, the Cuban regime might fall. In the end, it might be the Cubans who shy away from an end to the embargo. The Americans have little to lose either way.

But that is all politics. The important thing to understand about Cuba is the historic U.S. obsession with the island, and why the Cubans have never been able to find their balance with the United States. The answer lies in geopolitics. The politics in play now are simply the bubble on the surface of much deeper forces.

"There are serious doubts about the fairness and impartiality of [the Cuban Five's] trial which have not been resolved on appeal."

The Trial of the Cuban Five Was Unjust

Amnesty International

Amnesty International (AI) is an international human rights organization. In the following viewpoint, it reports on the case of the Cuban Five, a group of five men convicted of spying in the United States for Cuba. AI says these men may not have been granted a fair trial. AI says that holding the trial in Miami, where sentiment was strongly against the men, made it difficult to select unbiased jurors. In addition, AI says the United States refused to give the defense certain evidence for security reasons. AI also argues that the US decision to prevent two of the Cuban Five from seeing their wives while in prison is a violation of human rights.

As you read, consider the following questions:

1. According to AI, what is the WASP network?

2. On what three grounds did the UN working group argue that the Cuban Five had not been granted a fair trial?

3. According to AI, when did Adriana Pérez and Olga Alanueva last see their husbands?

This [viewpoint] describes Amnesty International's concerns about the fairness of the trial of five men imprisoned in the USA since 1998 on charges related to their activities as intelligence agents for the Cuban government. The men, known as the Cuban Five, are Cuban nationals Fernando González (aka [also know as] Ruben Campa), Gerardo Hernández and Ramón Labañino (aka Luis Medina), and US nationals Antonio Guerrero and René González. All are serving long prison sentences in US federal prisons.

Convicted of Espionage

The five are reported to have been among a group of intelligence agents known as the Wasp Network (La Red Avispa), headed by Cuba's Directorate of Intelligence, which infiltrated Cuban-American groups in Florida who support regime change in Cuba. They were arrested in September 1998 and charged with conspiring to act as unregistered agents of the Republic of Cuba, and related offences. At their trial, the US government alleged that, as well as monitoring anti-Castro [referring to Cuban leader Fidel Castro] groups, the Wasp Network reported to Cuba about the operation of US military facilities, including the Key West Naval Air Station in Florida, where one of the five was employed as a labourer. Two of the five were alleged to have supervised attempts by other agents to penetrate the Miami facility of [US] Southern Command, which oversees operations of US military forces in Latin America and the Caribbean.

After a lengthy pretrial detention, and a jury trial before the federal district court in Miami, Florida, lasting nearly seven months, the five were convicted in June 2001 on a combined total of 26 counts. These included acting and conspiring to act as unregistered agents of a foreign government; fraud and misuse of identity documents; and, in the case of three of the accused, conspiracy to gather and transmit national defence information. The men were sentenced in December 2001 to prison terms ranging from 15 years to life.

As well as being sentenced to life imprisonment for conspiracy to gather and transmit national defence information, Gerardo Hernández received a second life prison sentence for conspiracy to murder. This was based on his alleged role in the shooting down by Cuba of two planes operated by the US anti-Castro organization "Brothers to the Rescue" (BTTR), in 1996, in which four people died.

The defendants have not denied acting as unregistered agents for the Cuban government. However, they have denied the most serious charges against them and contend that their role was to focus on Cuban exile groups responsible for hostile acts against Cuba, and visible signs of US military action towards Cuba, rather than to breach US national security. No evidence was presented against them at trial to show that the accused had actually handled or transmitted a single classified document or piece of information, although the US government contended that this was their intention.

Change of Location

In August 2005, a three-judge panel of the US Court of Appeals for the 11th Circuit unanimously overturned the convictions of the five on finding that pervasive community prejudice against the Castro government in the trial venire of Miami-Dade County merged with other factors to prejudice their right to a fair trial. The court ordered a new trial outside Miami. The decision was appealed by the US government and subsequently reversed in August 2006 by the full (*en banc*) Court of Appeal, by a 10–2 majority.

In June 2008, a three-judge panel of the 11th Circuit Court of Appeals ruled on other grounds of appeal which had been pending in the case. It upheld the convictions in all five cases but vacated part of the sentences imposed on three of the defendants on finding that they had been wrongly enhanced under federal sentencing guidelines. The decision vacated the life sentences imposed on Ramón Labañino and Antonio Guerrero for conspiracy to gather and transmit national defence information, as no top-secret information had in fact been gathered or transmitted. Ramón Labañino was subsequently resentenced to 30 years on that charge and Antonio Guerrero to 21 years and 10 months, both to be served concurrently with sentences on other counts. Fernando González had his sentence reduced from 19 years to 17 years and nine months, on the ground that the portion of his original sentence imposed for identity fraud had been set too high.

The court found that Gerardo Hernández's life sentence for conspiracy to gather and transmit national defence information had also been wrongly enhanced on the same grounds as in Labañino and Guerrero's cases. However, it declined to remand him for resentencing on the ground that, as he was already serving a life sentence for conspiracy to murder, any error in the recalculation of his sentence on the other charge was "irrelevant to the time he will serve in prison". Gerardo Hernández is the only one of the five still serving life in prison. He is serving two terms of life imprisonment, plus 15 years, to be served concurrently.

The June 2008 decision to uphold the convictions was not unanimous. One of the three judges, Judge Kravitz, dissented from the decision to uphold the conspiracy to murder conviction in the case of Gerardo Hernández on the ground that, in her view, the government had failed to prove beyond a reasonable doubt that he had entered into an agreement to shoot down the BTTR planes in international airspace and kill the occupants.

Judge Birch concurred with the court's opinion on all matters before it, while admitting that the issue raised in the conspiracy to murder conviction "presents a very close case". He also took the opportunity to reiterate his opinion (set out in his dissent to the en banc appeal court's August 2006 decision on the trial venue) that "the motion for change of venue should have been granted", stating that the defendants "were subjected to such a degree of harm based upon demonstrated pervasive community prejudice that their convictions should have been reversed".

In June 2009 the US Supreme Court denied a petition for leave to appeal against the convictions of the five without giving reasons.

In June 2010, lawyers for the five filed a further motion in the district (trial) court, seeking habeas corpus [the right of a person under arrest to be brought before the court] relief on the basis of new issues. These include a claim of ineffective assistance of counsel in the case of Gerardo Hernández, and new evidence of alleged government misconduct in the case. The latter claim is based on newly discovered evidence that journalists who had written prejudicial articles in Miami against Cuba at the time of the trial were paid employees of the US government as part of their work for anti-Castro media outlets, Radio Martí and TV Martí. A hearing on these issues had not yet taken place at the time of writing.

The United Nations Working Group on Arbitrary Detention

In May 2005, the UN [United Nations] Working Group on Arbitrary Detention adopted an opinion on the case in which it concluded that US government had failed to guarantee the Cuban Five a fair trial under Article 14 of the International Covenant on Civil and Political Rights (ICCPR), a treaty the USA has ratified. While noting that the case was still pending before the US appeal courts, the working group stated that its

The Cinco Heroes

The "Cuban Five," known in Cuba as the *Cinco Heroes*, are counterintelligence agents and spies, sent by the [Fidel] Castro government to infiltrate several Miami-based exile groups in the 1990s. Based on their work, the Cuban government passed information to the [Bill] Clinton administration's State Department and directly to an FBI [Federal Bureau of Investigation] team that visited Havana to investigate the alleged plans of those groups under surveillance to commit terrorist attacks against Cuba. In the fall of 1998, the FBI subsequently arrested the five Cuban informants, charging them with a variety of crimes, from falsifying documents to conspiracy to commit espionage. Between the arrest and the beginning of their trial, the five spent almost three years in jail, including 17 months in solitary confinement. In June 2001, all were found guilty. In December of that year, three were given life sentences; the other two, shorter terms between 15 and 19 years.

Until the Cuban Five were sentenced, Cuban officials did not move aggressively to bring sustained public and international attention to the case. Coinciding with the launch of the [George W.] Bush administration's "war on terror," their sentencing gave Cuba an appropriate context and trigger to do so. Havana argued that the five agents had been carrying out a patriotic duty to defend their homeland against attack in a country with a long history of tolerating and at times supporting exile extremists and terrorists. In this way, the Cuban government impugned the Bush administration's commitment to fighting terror as disingenuous and selective.

Julia E. Sweig, Cuba: What Everyone Needs to Know. New York: Oxford University Press, 2009.

findings were made on the basis of the facts and circumstances described, the responses received from the US government and further comments by the complaint's source.

The working group based its opinion on three factors, including the prejudicial impact of holding the trial in Miami. It also found that keeping the defendants in solitary confinement for part of their lengthy pretrial detention, during which they allegedly had limited access to their attorneys and to evidence, and classifying all documents in the case as "secret", weakened the possibilities of an adequate defence and "undermined the equal balance between the prosecution and the defense". Taking into account the severe sentences imposed, the working group concluded that the factors cited above, "combined together, are of such gravity that they confer the deprivation of liberty of these five persons an arbitrary character". It called on the government to adopt the necessary steps to remedy the situation.

The US government responded to the opinion by letter dated 6 September 2005, expressing its disappointment that the working group had issued its opinion while the matter was under active judicial review and pending appeal in the United States at that time. In reporting on the response in its annual report, the working group noted that the doctrine of exhaustion of domestic remedy did not apply as a criterion for the admissibility of its communications to governments when investigating cases of alleged arbitrary deprivation of liberty.

Summary of Amnesty International's Concerns

Amnesty International takes no position on whether the Cuban Five are guilty or innocent of the charges for which they have been convicted. However, having reviewed the case extensively over a number of years, the organization believes that there are serious doubts about the fairness and impartiality of their trial which have not been resolved on appeal.

Amnesty International's concerns are based on a combination of factors. A central, underlying concern relates to the fairness of holding the trial in Miami, given the pervasive community hostility toward the Cuban government in the area and media and other events which took place before and during the trial. There is evidence to suggest that these factors made it impossible to ensure a wholly impartial jury, despite the efforts of the trial judge in this regard. The right to a trial by a competent, independent and impartial tribunal is guaranteed under Article 10 of the Universal Declaration of Human Rights (UDHR) and Article 14 of the ICCPR, and is fundamental to the right to a fair trial. In order for such a right to be guaranteed, every trial must not only be fair but also be seen to be fair. As described in more detail below, there is serious doubt that this principle was fulfilled in this case. Amnesty International is concerned that the Supreme Court declined to hear the appeal on this and several other key issues in the case, despite the fact that judicial opinion in the lower courts has been deeply divided.

Amnesty International also shares the concern of the Working Group [on] Arbitrary Detention that the conditions under which the defence attorneys were allowed access to their clients, and to evidence, during pretrial investigations may have undermined the fundamental principle of "equality of arms" and the right of every defendant to have adequate facilities for the preparation of their defence. Although these issues were not grounds of appeal, it is one factor among others which raises concern about the overall fairness with which the defendants have been treated.

Amnesty International is further concerned about the strength of the evidence on which Gerardo Hernández was convicted of conspiracy to murder: an issue which was a ground of appeal to the US Supreme Court and which the court declined to review. Although Amnesty International is not in a position to second-guess the facts on which the jury reached its verdict, it believes that there are questions as to whether the government discharged its burden of proof that Hernández planned a shoot down of BTTR planes in international airspace, and thus within US jurisdiction, which was a necessary element of the charge against him. One essential guarantee of a fair trial is that a person charged with a criminal offence must be presumed innocent until the charge has been proved beyond a reasonable doubt. The UN Human Rights Committee (the ICCPR treaty monitoring body) has noted that, "Deviating from fundamental principles of fair trial, including the presumption of innocence, is prohibited at all times."

Given these concerns, and the lengthy sentences imposed, should further legal appeals on these issues be exhausted or carry little prospect of relief, Amnesty International calls on the US government to review the case and to take appropriate action to remedy any injustice.

Ban on Visits with Wives of Two of the Prisoners

For several years, Amnesty International has raised concern about the US government's denial of visas to allow the Cuban wives of Gerardo Hernández and René González to visit them in prison. Adriana Pérez has not seen her husband, Gerardo Hernández, since his arrest in 1998. Olga Salanueva, the wife of René González, has not seen her husband since the eve of his trial in November 2000. The US government has denied the visits on foreign policy and national security grounds, including, reportedly, on the alleged ground that the women were associated with the Wasp Network. Neither of the women has been charged with any crime in the USA and Olga Salanueva, who was a lawful permanent resident in the USA at the time of her husband's arrest, continued to live legally in the

USA for two and a half years during pretrial proceedings against her husband. She alleges that he was offered a plea bargain in which she would have been allowed to remain in the USA if he pleaded guilty; he refused and she was deported in November 2000 and is now deemed permanently ineligible to enter the USA.

Both women have made repeated applications to the US government for temporary visas to allow them to visit their husbands, with undertakings to abide by any security conditions deemed necessary. Their applications have been turned down, with the US authorities at times giving different grounds for the refusal of visas, citing various sections of immigration, national security and border protection legislation. No detailed reasons have been provided to either of the women for the continued denial of visas. At one point, in 2002, Adriana Pérez was actually granted a visa but was detained for 11 hours at a Houston airport, after which her visa was revoked and she was refused entry to the USA.

Amnesty International has repeatedly expressed concern to the US government that the blanket, and apparently permanent, bar on the men receiving visits from their wives, without due consideration of any conditions that might make such visits possible, is unnecessarily punitive and contrary to standards for the humane treatment of prisoners and states' obligation to protect family life. This is of special concern given the long prison sentences imposed, including the double life sentence in the case of Gerardo Hernández. Amnesty International continues to urge the government to grant the wives temporary visas on humanitarian grounds, under conditions that would meet security concerns. Visas have been granted for other relatives in Cuba to visit the five prisoners occasionally, although there have reportedly been delays or difficulties at times. According to court documents, all of the five men have exemplary behavioural records in prison.

> *"Five have been tried and found guilty in court for criminal conspiracy in the murder of the Brothers to the Rescue pilots."*

The Imprisonment of the Cuban Five Is Just

Matt Lawrence and Thomas Van Hare

Matt Lawrence is president of Paratus International, a disaster-preparedness consulting firm. Thomas Van Hare is a former chairman of Freedom Flight International, a company involved in development and sales overseas of sophisticated military aircraft, and a former pilot for Brothers to the Rescue. In the following viewpoint, they say that Cuban American pilots were shot down and killed in 1996 on orders of Fidel Castro. They argue that the Cuban Five and other spies were implicated in these killings. The authors conclude that the Cuban Five were rightfully convicted of involvement in murder and that their imprisonment is just.

As you read, consider the following questions:

1. Who is Colonel Emilio Palacios, and why do the authors say he is implicated in the murder of the Brothers to the Rescue pilots?

2. How do the authors say that Raúl Castro has recast the Cuban Five by offering to trade them for the release of political prisoners?

3. Who was Ana Belen Montes, according to the viewpoint?

Unraveling the true story of what happened on February 24, 1996 [when four Cuban American pilots were shot down by Cuban fighter jets], is a difficult, confusing and challenging task. Without a doubt, through an extraordinarily extensive disinformation and influence campaign, Cuban intelligence has attempted to distort virtually everything related to the case—including the content and conclusions of many official U.S. documents. Yet what is known and what can be confirmed are nothing short of incredible.

Murdered Pilots

Four pilots are dead and their families still grieve. The families of Armando Alejandre Jr., Carlos Costa, Mario de la Peña and Pablo Morales will forever feel their loss.

That they were killed on the order of [Cuban leader] Fidel Castro himself is not in doubt, nor are the names of those responsible for the act itself—including the commander of the Cuban Air Force, General Rubén Martinez Puente, who personally gave the order to fire. The two pilots involved, El Teniente (LTC) Colonel Lorenzo Alberto Perez Perez and his brother and co-pilot, El Teniente Colonel (LTC) Francisco Perez Perez, murdered the four Brothers[1] pilots. Cuban Air Force pilot, El Teniente (LTC) Colonel Emilio Palacios who flew air cover for them and, it is worth noting, excitedly also asked for permission to fire. Yet according to one witness, one additional pilot reportedly helped them prepare for their mis-

1. Brothers to the Rescue is a Miami-based humanitarian organization which flew planes to assist refugees fleeing from Cuba. Cuba accused them of violating Cuban air space and of terrorist acts.

sion by flying a light aircraft to play the role of the Brothers to the Rescue planes for practice runs. His name is Adolfo Perez Pantoja—and he has never been indicted for his role in helping to prepare and train the pilots for the shoot down.

No doubt, there are dozens of others within Cuba, as members of the Cuban Air Force fighter squadron, as personnel manning various radar sites along the coast, and as Cuban air traffic controllers, who played a part in what the U.S. government has categorically defined, in courtroom proceedings, as nothing less than *murder*. They each share the guilt, and perhaps many of them are still proud of their role.

Cuban Spies

Additionally, there are at least six Cuban spies involved who were on U.S. soil. Five have been tried and found guilty in court for criminal conspiracy in the murder of the Brothers to the Rescue pilots. Since their conviction, despite years of legal wrangling and appeals, they remain in jail, *guilty beyond a reasonable doubt*. Their names are Antonio Guerrero, René González, Gerardo Hernández, Luis Medina (aka [also known as] Ramón Labañino Salazar), and Orlando Campo (aka Ruben Campa and/or Fernando González). Together, they are known as the Cuban Five, and their ongoing incarceration is a matter of public spectacle and great propaganda value for Cuba's domestic scene.

Even as the new [Barack] Obama administration was being sworn in in January 2009, the Cuban government has attempted to yet again recast the Cuban Five to new purposes. By offering to trade them for the release of political prisoners at home, [Cuban president] Raúl Castro, who was also personally involved in the murder, has established the release of these convicted criminals as a seemingly innocuous precondition to improving relations between Washington and Havana.

A seventh spy, Juan Pablo Roque, who was Cuba's key man in planning and undertaking the mission itself, remains a free man, living in Cuba. He left behind his "cover," a wife and a son in South Florida, who are daily cognizant of his ultimate betrayal to them as well.

An eighth spy was involved, one who could be called the "Queen of Spies," Ana Belen Montes, the DIA's [Defense Intelligence Agency's] and the U.S. intelligence community's top Cuba briefer. Her mission involved as much stealing of secrets as it did in inventing false ones. Over her decade and a half of involvement spying for Cuba, she not only provided a voluminous amount of highly classified military and political information to the Cubans, but also personally maneuvered U.S. government and U.S. military policies to conclusions that had been, quite literally, dictated by Fidel Castro. It is not a far stretch of the imagination to realize that she was almost certainly instrumental in breaking down the relationship between the U.S. government and the Brothers to the Rescue group, in redefining Cuban defectors as little more than "migrants" in line with those coming to the U.S.A. as illegal immigrants, to create and modify the U.S. response to the shoot down itself, to rewrite post–shoot down studies, and to stifle dissent among other U.S. intelligence officers studying Cuban affairs.

She briefed everyone from top generals to congressmen, and even to the White House, on what had happened, ensuring that the data was slanted to favor Cuba's ongoing disinformation and influence campaigns. It is astonishing that just two years after the shoot down, Montes had even managed to convince many that Cuba was no longer a threat to the United States.

For Cuba, these spies are considered nothing less than national heroes. For the United States, they are little more than convicted conspirators who were directly responsible for the murder of four people, three of which were U.S. citizens and one a permanent U.S. resident.

Periodical and Internet Sources Bibliography

The following articles have been selected to supplement the diverse views presented in this chapter.

Lizette Alvarez	"Pull of Family Reshapes U.S.-Cuban Relations," *New York Times*, November 21, 2011.
José R. Cárdenas	"The Phony Cuba Embargo Debate," *Shadow Government* (blog), *Foreign Policy*, March 21, 2012. http://shadow.foreignpolicy.com.
Damien Cave	"One of 'Cuban Five' Spies Is Released on Probation," *New York Times*, October 7, 2011.
CBS Baltimore	"Cuba Proposes U.S. Release Cuban 5 in Exchange for Alan Gross," May 10, 2012. http://baltimore.cbslocal.com.
Jeffrey Goldberg	"America's Absurd and Self-Defeating Cuba Policy," *Atlantic*, September 16, 2010.
Jonathan M. Hansen	"Give Guantánamo Back to Cuba," *New York Times*, January 10, 2012.
Harvey Mackay	"Mackay: U.S. Companies Pay Price for Cuba Embargo," *Columbus Business First*, March 18, 2012.
Jonathan Masters	"Closing Guantanamo?," Council on Foreign Relations, November 9, 2011. www.cfr.org.
Tim Padgett	"The Oil Off Cuba: Washington and Havana Dance at Arms Length over Spill Prevention," *Time*, January 27, 2012.
Michael Orion Powell	"Cuba: Change Is Not One Sided," *The Foundry* (blog), Heritage Foundation, April 3, 2010. http://blog.heritage.org.
Ginger Thompson	"Restrictions on Travel to Cuba Are Eased," *New York Times*, January 14, 2011.

For Further Discussion

Chapter 1

1. Based on the viewpoints in this chapter, does the Cuban government respect human rights? Explain your answer.

2. What evidence is there from this chapter that Cubans are dissatisfied with some aspects of their government? How does the government respond to this dissatisfaction? Explain your answers.

Chapter 2

1. Steve Brouwer discusses Cuban medical aid to Venezuela. Based on Jonathan Glennie's viewpoint in chapter 1, why is Cuba able to provide this aid?

2. Would Peter McKenna agree with Paul Richter's viewpoint suggesting that Cuban-Russian ties are a danger to the hemisphere? Explain your answer.

Chapter 3

1. Based on the viewpoints by Alex Leary and Benjamin G. Bishin and Casey A. Klofstad, what if anything could Democratic candidates do to appeal more strongly to the Cuban community? What if anything could Republican candidates do? Explain your answers.

Chapter 4

1. Based on the viewpoints in this chapter, do you think it is wrong for foreign policy decisions to be based on domestic political considerations? Why or why not?

2. Do you think George Friedman would agree with Julia E. Sweig that the United States should give Guantánamo Bay back to Cuba? Why or why not? Explain your answer.

2. Do the actions of the Cuban Five support the maintaining of a Cuban embargo? Do they support the dismantling of the embargo? Or are they completely unrelated to the embargo? Explain your answer.

Organizations to Contact

The editors have compiled the following list of organizations concerned with the issues debated in this book. The descriptions are derived from materials provided by the organizations. All have publications or information available for interested readers. The list was compiled on the date of publication of the present volume; the information provided here may change. Be aware that many organizations take several weeks or longer to respond to inquiries, so allow as much time as possible.

Association for the Study of the Cuban Economy (ASCE)
PO Box 28267, Washington, DC   20038-8267
e-mail: asce@ascecuba.org
website: www.ascecuba.org

The Association for the Study of the Cuban Economy (ASCE) is a nonprofit and nonpolitical professional organization. Affiliated with the American Economic Association and the Allied Social Sciences Association, the ASCE maintains professional contacts with social scientists throughout the world who are interested in engaging in scholarly discussion and research on Cuba and its comparative development. The ASCE regularly publishes a newsletter, and its website also includes downloadable special studies and occasional papers.

CATO Institute
1000 Massachusetts Avenue NW
Washington, DC   20001-5403
(202) 842-0200 • fax: (202) 842-3490
website: www.cato.org

The Cato Institute is a nonpartisan libertarian public policy research foundation that promotes the principles of limited government, individual liberty, and peace. The institute regularly publishes policy analysis reports and op-eds that focus on foreign policy and trade issues involving Cuba, such as "Freedom and Exchange with Communist Cuba" and "Rethinking the US Embargo Against Cuba."

Council on Foreign Relations (CFR)

The Harold Pratt House, New York, NY   10065
(212) 434-9400 • fax: (212) 434-9800
e-mail: communications@cfr.org
website: www.cfr.org

The Council on Foreign Relations (CFR) is an independent, nonpartisan membership organization, think tank, and publisher. CFR researches the international aspects of American economic and political policies. Its journal *Foreign Affairs*, published six times a year, provides analysis on global situations including those pertaining to Cuba.

Heritage Foundation

214 Massachusetts Avenue NE, Washington, DC   20002-4999
(202) 546-4400 • fax: (202) 546-8328
e-mail: info@heritage.org
website: www.heritage.org

The Heritage Foundation is a conservative think tank that formulates and promotes public policies based on the principles of free enterprise, limited government, individual freedom, traditional American values, and a strong national defense. It publishes many position papers on US-Cuban policy, including "Cuba's Lost History" and "What Wilman Villar's Tragic Death Tells Us About Today's Cuba."

Human Rights Watch (HRW)

350 Fifth Avenue, 34th Floor, New York, NY   10118-3299
(212) 290-4700 • fax: (212) 736-1300
website: www.hrw.org

Human Rights Watch (HRW) is dedicated to protecting the human rights of people around the world to prevent discrimination, uphold political freedom, protect people from inhumane conduct in wartime, and bring offenders to justice. Human Rights Watch investigates and exposes human rights violations and holds abusers accountable. Its website includes an overview of human rights issues in Cuba and numerous other press releases, letters, and articles regarding human rights in Cuba.

Institute for Cuban and Cuban-American Studies (ICCAS)

1531 Brescia Avenue, PO Box 248174
Coral Gables, FL   33124-3010
(305) 284-2822 • fax: (305) 284-4875
e-mail: iccas@miami.edu
website: www6.miami.edu/iccas/iccas.htm

The Institute for Cuban and Cuban-American Studies (ICCAS) is part of the University of Miami. ICCAS serves as a world-class academic center for the research and study of Cuban and Cuban American topics. It organizes seminars and lectures, publishes academic research, and offers a special summer program on Cuba for US and foreign students.

Institute for Policy Studies (IPS)

1112 Sixteenth Street NW, Suite 600, Washington, DC   20036
(202) 234-9382
e-mail: info@ips-dc.org
website: www.ips-dc.org

The Institute for Policy Studies (IPS) is a community of public scholars and organizers linking peace, justice, and the environment in the United States and around the world. A progressive multi-issue think tank, IPS works with social movements to promote democracy and challenge concentrated wealth, corporate influence, and military power. The institute publishes *Foreign Policy in Focus*, which has briefings and reports on Cuba, including "Cuba's Culture of Dissent" and "Review: Cuba Since the Revolution of 1959."

Latin America Working Group (LAWG)

424 C Street NE, Washington, DC   20002
(202) 546-7010
e-mail: lawg@lawg.org
website: www.lawg.org

The Latin America Working Group (LAWG) is a US coalition dedicated to foreign policy. The Latin America Working Group and its sister organization, the Latin America Working Group

Education Fund, carry out the coalition's mission to encourage US policies toward Latin America that promote human rights, justice, peace, and sustainable development, including in Cuba. LAWG publishes the *Advocate*, which is available on its website, along with numerous policy articles.

United States Department of State
2201 C Street NW, Washington, DC   20520
(202) 647-4000
website: www.state.gov

The Department of State is a US federal agency that advises the president on issues of foreign policy. The department aims to "shape and sustain a peaceful, prosperous, just, and democratic world and foster conditions for stability and progress for the benefit of the American people and people everywhere," according to its mission statement. The department website includes a section on "Countries & Regions" that provides a great deal of information about the country of Cuba, including a fact sheet about bilateral US-Cuban relations, news articles, and publications such as "The Path to Freedom: Countering Repression and Strengthening Civil Society in Cuba."

Washington Office on Latin America (WOLA)
1666 Connecticut Avenue NW, Suite 400
Washington, DC   20009
(202) 797-2171
website: www.wola.org

The Washington Office on Latin America (WOLA) is committed to promoting human rights, democracy, and social justice by working with partners in Latin America and the Caribbean to shape policies in the United States and abroad. WOLA publishes a number of resource guides on Cuba, and the website contains news articles and analysis of Cuban policy.

Bibliography of Books

Harlan Abrahams and Arturo Lopez-Levy
Raúl Castro and the New Cuba: A Close-Up View of Change. Jefferson, NC: McFarland & Company, 2011.

Keith Bolender
Voices from the Other Side: An Oral History of Terrorism Against Cuba. New York: Pluto Press, 2010.

Fidel Castro and Ignacio Ramonet
Fidel Castro, My Life: A Spoken Autobiography. Trans. Andrew Hurley. New York: Scribner, 2009.

Aviva Chomsky
A History of the Cuban Revolution. Malden, MA: Wiley-Blackwell, 2011.

Aviva Chomsky, Barry Carr, Pamela Maria Smorkaloff, eds.
The Cuba Reader: History, Culture, Politics. Durham, NC: Duke University Press, 2003.

Leycester Coltman
The Real Fidel Castro. New Haven, CT: Yale University Press, 2005.

Jorge I. Dominguez, Rafael Hernandez, and Lorena G. Barberia, eds.
Debating U.S.-Cuban Relations: Shall We Play Ball? New York: Routledge, 2012.

Daniel P. Erikson
The Cuba Wars: Fidel Castro, the United States, and the Next Revolution. New York: Bloomsbury Press, 2008.

Reese Erlich   *Dateline Havana: The Real Story of U.S. Policy and the Future of Cuba.* Sausalito, CA: PoliPointPress, 2009.

Edward J. Gonzalez   *Cuban Exiles on the Trade Embargo: Interviews.* Jefferson, NC: McFarland, 2007.

Guillermo J. Grenier and Lisandro Pérez   *The Legacy of Exile: Cubans in the United States.* Boston, MA: Allyn & Bacon, 2003.

Sergio Guerra-Vilaboy and Oscar Loyola-Vega   *Cuba: A History.* New York: Ocean Press, 2010.

Patrick J. Haney and Walt Vanderbush   *The Cuban Embargo: The Domestic Politics of American Foreign Policy.* Pittsburgh, PA: University of Pittsburgh Press, 2005.

Jonathan M. Hansen   *Guantánamo: An American History.* New York: Hill and Wang, 2011.

Hal Klepak   *Raúl Castro and Cuba: A Military Story.* New York: Palgrave Macmillan, 2012.

Brian Latell   *After Fidel: The Inside Story of Castro's Regime and Cuba's Next Leader.* New York: Palgrave Macmillan, 2005.

Jeanne Parr Lemkau and David L. Strug   *Love, Loss and Longing: The Impact of U.S. Travel Policy on Cuban-American Families.* Washington, DC: Latin American Working Group Education Fund, 2007.

Yoani Sánchez	*Havana Real: One Woman Fights to Tell the Truth About Cuba Today.* Brooklyn, NY: Melville House, 2011.
Lars Schoultz	*That Infernal Little Cuban Republic: The United States and the Cuban Revolution.* Chapel Hill: University of North Carolina Press, 2009.
Stephen Irving Max Schwab	*Guantánamo, USA: The Untold History of America's Cuban Outpost.* Lawrence: University Press of Kansas, 2009.
Paolo Spadoni	*Failed Sanctions: Why the U.S. Embargo Against Cuba Could Never Work.* Gainesville: University Press of Florida, 2010.
Clifford L. Staten	*The History of Cuba.* Westport, CT: Greenwood Press, 2003.
Julia E. Sweig	*Cuba: What Everyone Needs to Know.* New York: Oxford University Press, 2009.
Julia E. Sweig	*Inside the Cuban Revolution: Fidel Castro and the Urban Underground.* Cambridge, MA: Harvard University Press, 2002.
Armando Valladares	*Against All Hope: A Memoir of Life in Castro's Gulag.* San Francisco, CA: Encounter Books, 2001.

Index